True revivalists are rare to f nitely the voice of a revivalist. L, with this urgent message found in *Death to Counterfeit Christianity.* She is a product of major revivals in this nation, so her voice carries authority in this area. You will be challenged to dig deeper and reach higher in your pursuit of Jesus. Your spiritual hunger, prayer, and worship will be stretched and equipped by her great revelation and insight. Lydia knows what it takes to bring revival. As you read, be ready to be gripped by the presence of the Lord and forever changed!

Thank you, Lydia, for this timely message.

PAUL AND KIM OWENS
Senior Leaders
Fresh Start Church, Peoria, AZ

Lydia Marrow is a true revivalist and a mighty voice of power and clarity in the earth today. This book is a true clarion call for the genuine church to arise in the earth releasing salvation, truth, hope and victory!

APOSTLE JIM RALEY
Senior Leader,Calvary Christian Center,
Ormond Beach, FL

This book will set your heart on fire and prepare you to be a catalyst for revival because Lydia Marrow's life and ministry was forged in revival fire. Her passion for revival is clearly manifested in her anointed worship and preaching and writing. She hits the nail on the head when she emphasizes that revival must first and foremost take place in the heart of a person in response to the hunger God creates. This book will give you a hunger for God's glory in your personal life and church that will lead to you to deep repentance. The subject of revival is often linked to "mega meetings" and "mega leaders." One of the notable features of Lydia's book is the pastoral language that she uses. For revival to be sustainable, it must impact the local church. Anyone and any church can expect a God-sent revival. You will not be the same after reading this book. Read it prayerfully, meditatively; preach from it and share the message with others.

Rev. Ong Sek Leang
General Superintendent
Assemblies of God of Malaysia

Lydia has released a powerful and much-needed word for this age! I was overwhelmed with excitement and hope as I scanned the pages of this book, Lydia's illustration and definition of revival, stopped me from reading and drove me to prayer!

"God wants to close the gap" is still ringing in my ears! Lydia's passion for revival and her statements; "I am aware of this fact: we owe the next generation a move of God," and "God wants to put His name, His reputation, back on His Church," caused the fire in my heart to run hot with excitement, and brought a surge of hope into my spirit! *Death to Counterfeit Christianity* is a must read and one to put into every hand of those around you; it will challenge the reader and cause them to take hold of the call for Revival.

Apostle Keith E. Taylor
Senior Pastor, Cross Tabernacle Church
Founder of Gilgal Ministries

Lydia Marrow's *Death to Counterfeit Christianity* will challenge you to the core of your soul. We have known Lydia for several years, and she is a firebrand who calls the Church to the pursuit for revival! Every time she has ministered at our churches and conferences, lives are radically changed!

In this book, Lydia will share with you vital keys to living your life on fire for God. You will not want to be a lukewarm, compromised Christian living a mediocre life— if you will let her words break your heart and drive you to your knees.

We are honored to partner with her, Nathan, and the entire Vanguard team in calling the remnant into action! Lydia is the real deal! She lives what she preaches. And that's why we are proud to be her friends. Buckle your seat belt—you are never going to be the same!

Jody and Lanora Morin
FountainGate Ministries International

This book is like a voice crying out in the wilderness to hungry remnant revivalists saying, "Anyone who is thirsty, come and drink!" *Death to Counterfeit Christianity* will bring life to its readers as it is a smartly written and anointed book. The personal stories and life-changing revelation will inspire you and keep you reading until the end.

Apostle Randall Burton
Senior Leader, Northview Church
Columbus, IN

DEATH TO COUNTERFEIT CHRISTIANITY

BECOME THE REVIVAL REMNANT THAT RELEASES
OPEN HEAVENS THROUGH PRAYER

Lydia S. Marrow

Please note that Destiny Image's publishing style capitalizes certain pronouns that refer to the Father, Son, and Holy Spirit, and may differ from some publishers' styles. Take note that the name satan and related names are not capitalized. We choose not to acknowledge him, even to the point of violating grammatical rules.

DESTINY IMAGE® PUBLISHERS, INC.
P.O. Box 310, Shippensburg, PA 17257-0310
"Promoting Inspired Lives."

This book and all other Destiny Image and Destiny Image Fiction books are available at Christian bookstores and distributors worldwide.

For more information on foreign distributors, call 717-532-3040.
Reach us on the Internet: www.destinyimage.com.

ISBN 13 TP: 978-0-7684-7232-5
ISBN 13 eBook: 978-0-7684-7233-2

For Worldwide Distribution, Printed in Columbia
1 2 3 4 5 6 7 8 / 27 26 25 24 23

ACKNOWLEDGMENTS

First, I want to thank my husband, Nathan Marrow. He believed in this book and its message long before I did, and he has been my greatest encourager. Nath, I am so glad I got to marry my best friend, and I'm so glad we are contending for revival together. I love you!

I want to thank Mom and Dad. You raised us to love Jesus and His people, and you provided opportunities for us to minister in the church long before that was a good idea. You led us so well, and I am so grateful. Thank you for your determination to take us to revival and to keep the fires burning.

My extended family, both American and British, I love you all so very much. I don't know how I've been so blessed to have such an amazing tribe, such a wonderful support system. I love you all, and I thank God for you.

I want to thank the Vanguard Ministries team. I cannot tell you what it has meant to serve on the frontlines with you. There is no other group of people I would rather serve with. We have walked through fire together, and we have seen God do what only He can do. I love each of you, and I am so glad that we became adopted cousins. I especially want to thank Kim for being so wonderful to my boys. You are a wonderful Mimi, and I would never have gotten this book completed without you.

Pastor Lindell Cooley, I am so thankful for you. You demonstrated what revival worship is supposed to look like during the years of the Brownsville Revival, but what is so rare and astonishing is this: you still embody that passion today. Thank you for pioneering vertical worship for this nation. Thank you for being such a wonderful mentor in my life.

Pastor John and Brenda Kilpatrick, I truly feel that I owe you my life. You have been a breathing demonstration of what loving the presence of God looks like. After all these years, you are still hungry, and you make me want more of Jesus. Thank you for allowing me to serve alongside you. Thank you for taking me in as a spiritual daughter. You have always believed in me, and your impact on my life is immeasurable.

DEDICATION

I would like to dedicate this book to my grandfather, the Rev. John F. Moore. His life of prayer and sacrifice were the backdrop for his leadership of our family and the church that he pastored for forty-six years. His prayer life has been a provocation to me, making me want to leave that kind of legacy for my children. I'm so grateful to have a heritage of revival!

CONTENTS

Foreword 1

Introduction 3

Chapter 1 It's Time to Mind the Gap 5

Chapter 2 Looking for a Ladder 33

Chapter 3 Refining or Redefining? 49

Chapter 4 The Manifestation of God's Reputation 63

Chapter 5 The Convergence: When Heaven and Earth Collide 81

Chapter 6 The Driving Force of Hunger 95

Chapter 7 Hosting the Holy 107

Chapter 8 Snake Voices: The Need for Discernment . . . 121

Chapter 9 It's Time to Shake It Up! 143

Chapter 10 The Unlikely Ones 159

Chapter 11 Having a Fearless Heart 181

FOREWORD

I REMEMBER VERY VIVIDLY the first time I met Lydia. I interviewed her at a Brownsville Revival service when she was eleven years old. I was taken aback by the level of maturity and confidence she exuded. She was a stand-out. I had never interviewed any child that was so comfortable in front of a huge crowd and had such a command in responding to my probing questions. The crowd loved her; she was a refreshing breath of air.

Later, I learned why Lydia embodied such great qualities. I came to know her grandfather, John Moore, and her entire family—therein was the key. Her grandfather was a stalwart man of faith and a southern gentleman. He was the patriarch of a great family, a tremendous leader, and a gatekeeper in the city of Augusta, Georgia, the home of the Masters Golf Tournament.

As Lydia matured, I found her to be a powerful psalmist and songwriter, a very gifted songwriter. Shortly after I founded Church of His Presence in Daphne, Alabama, I asked her to join my staff when she was only twenty-two years old. Lydia held even more surprises; she developed into a significant preacher.

Today, she is just as bold and confident as when I first met her. Now, she is the author of her first book. The title she has chosen is *Death to Counterfeit Christianity,* and you guessed right, it is a revival book.

When I think of Lydia Marrow, the first words that come to mind are bold, worshipper, and revivalist. Lydia will never be able to be anything other than be a revivalist. It is inbred in her by the Holy Spirit. She lives on the edge and does not know what a comfort zone is. She thrives on prayer, bold prayer, and bold preaching, and she lives in the faith zone! Her book is really an expression of what the Holy Spirit has put in her.

As I read the manuscript, it was evident she had written a wonderful book, and I am so proud of her. *Death to Counterfeit Christianity* is not only the title but also Lydia's mantra. I believe as you read this anointed book, filled with the Word of God and personal illustrations, you will hear the Holy Spirit speaking to you to make the necessary changes and adjustments in your life to go after God as never before.

REV. JOHN A. KILPATRICK
Founder and Executive Pastor, Church of His Presence
Daphne, Alabama

INTRODUCTION

AS THIS IS MY first book, I am quite certain that you may not be familiar with me. You may never have heard of me before in your life, and that is to be expected. I trust that as you read these pages, you will get to know me a little bit. But much more than that, I pray that as you read this book, you will be provoked to hunger for God like you never have before.

I am no one special. I don't know if I have any exceptional gifts to speak of. All that I am is a life on fire, a life that was touched by the One whose eyes burn like flames of fire. From the time that He first touched me until now, that fire burns in my spirit.

I did not choose to write this book so that you would become familiar with my ministry. I wrote this book to make you want to get down on your knees and cry out to God until He brands you with the fires of revival. The Jesus whom I encountered in March of 1996 wants to do for you what He did for me.

As we begin this journey together, allow me to let you in on a little secret: *authentic revival is always personal before it is corporate.* There have never been any shortcuts. Something must happen in your inner life before something can happen around you or through your ministry.

My husband, Nathan Marrow, and I launched Vanguard Ministries in July of 2021 with this specific mandate from God: we are called to be a holy provocation, to provoke the Church toward revival and the lost toward repentance. My prayer for you is that this book will serve as a provocation, stirring you for revival and igniting a fresh passion for Jesus. I am asking God to raise up people who will allow God to use their lives to provoke the sleeping Church awake, contending for revival in our time.

Before you go any further, would you do something for me? Would you ask the Holy Spirit to do that which He is famous for? Ask Him to reveal Jesus Christ in a way you have never seen Him before. Let Him do His work *in you*, and I promise you, on the authority of the Word of God, you will never be the same again.

Chapter 1

IT'S TIME TO MIND THE GAP

It will come about after this that I will pour out My Spirit on all mankind; and your sons and daughters will prophesy, your old men will dream dreams, your young men will see visions. Even on the male and female servants I will pour out My Spirit in those days (Joel 2:28-29).

I GREW UP IN Augusta, Georgia, the home of the Masters golf tournament and of the godfather of soul, James Brown. Augusta is a charming town that is not too small and not too big. It is not an extraordinary place at all. It has nice areas, it has not-so-nice areas, and mostly it has normal folks who are just living life.

Our home and our church were in one of the bad neighborhoods of town. It was a common experience for us to witness drug deals or to see prostitutes walking the streets, their eyes always looking all around to make sure they wouldn't get in trouble with their pimp. We often greeted them on the way to church.

It was common for people to walk into our services right off the street. My granddaddy was the pastor, and I can remember him praying for drunk people who had wandered into the church. By the time Granddaddy had finished praying the prayer of faith, they were saved, delivered, sober, and baptized in the Holy Spirit with the evidence of speaking in tongues. I thought this sort of thing was happening in everybody's church.

My granddaddy, John F. Moore, was the greatest man of God I have ever known in my life! His walk with God was so steady, and his prayer life was so remarkable. I can remember hearing him pray in the mornings when I would be at my grandparents' house, and the tangible presence of God would be so strong you could hardly breathe. I would walk into his den and see him in his favorite chair, cup of coffee in hand, praying in the Holy Ghost over his family and his church. Then, his phone would begin to ring. Everyone knew that Pastor Moore was up and praying, so they would call him for prayer. He was there for them, and so was the power of God.

Granddaddy was a man who moved in the miraculous quite a lot. He used to have what he called "The Friday Noon Prayer, Healing, and Miracle Service" every week. When I was a little girl, they would bring me along to the service. I sat on the communion table while the older saints would gather in the center of the altar and sing hymns acapella until they felt the Holy Spirit. Then, they would begin to pray for the sick. We saw cancer healed multiple times. It was just normal to see God reverse sickness and disease in those meetings, and then we would casually go out to eat for lunch at the local cafeteria. Granddaddy's faith was and is one of my greatest inspirations.

I wish I could say that the rest of us were just like him, but that just wasn't the case. To tell you the truth, the church had become so religious.

Now, I want to take a moment right here and tell you my personal definition of what religion is. Religion is when you think you know how to have church with or without the presence of the Holy Spirit. It's when you are willing to proclaim things publicly, but you don't allow yourself to live them out privately. It's when your life doesn't match your message.

None of us meant to become religious, and I'm sure it didn't happen overnight. I can remember "tarrying in the altar," when I was a little girl. I can remember moments when God's presence would come, but I can also remember the drudgery of the times when He didn't come, and no one really did anything about it. There was no pressing in, no real pursuit of His presence. We knew what songs to sing, what prayers to pray; we knew what was going to be preached, and we knew what time we would get out of church.

You know what? To tell you the truth, I was bored to tears. It was miserable to hear someone preach that Jesus saves and does miracles only to be disappointed with an empty altar.

You see, every person on the face of the earth is hungry for God, but many people are only filling themselves with spiritual appetite suppressants. That is why so many of our churches are filled with entertainment, which is nothing more than a cheap substitute for the presence of God. Religion will always try to keep you busy and entertained so that you won't notice how spiritually bankrupt you really are.

We had become trapped in a religious rut. My dad was Granddaddy's associate pastor, and he and Mom also were the worship leaders of the church. Dad had just led the church through a building program, and he was so burnt out. I can remember him talking about how frustrated he was because no one was getting saved. No one was really sharing Jesus. It was just church as usual.

In the midst of all that religion, sin issues began to creep up in the congregation. I don't want to embarrass anyone, so I won't be detailed about that, but neither can I act like everything was okay. It wasn't. And even as a young girl, I couldn't help but notice that the people who were in sin were also singing the songs, praying the prayers, and dropping money in the offering bag. How could someone play the church game when they knew that they were not right with God? How does that happen? How can you lie about who you really are and lift your hands to praise the Lord?

Religion will always tell you that you're the special one. It's not okay for others to do certain things, but you can do whatever you want because you have needs.

I have noticed that religion will always produce boredom with God, but just as significantly, it will always produce a cover-up for moral corruption.

We were in a place where something was going to have to give. We had become so dead in religion. We needed something, and I'm not sure anyone really knew what it was.

It was early in 1996 when one of my dad's pastor friends gave him a call. He said, "There's this revival happening in Pensacola, Florida, at a church called Brownsville Assembly of God. People are shaking and falling out under the power of God."

Dad said, "I wouldn't cross the street to see that." He had grown up in a Pentecostal church, and he loved the legitimate moving of the Holy Spirit, but he was not easily impressed by physical manifestations. Anyone can fake a physical manifestation. He needed something more than that.

His friend responded, "Well, the revival has only been going on since Father's Day 1995, and so far between 5,000 and 6,000 people have gotten saved."

Dad immediately said, "We're going."

We all loaded up in our Ford Aerostar minivan to make our first trip to the Brownsville Revival. Keep in mind, Augusta, Georgia, to Pensacola, Florida, is nearly a 500-mile trip. When you get hungry enough, you become willing to go to a place where someone has set a table for you, and inconvenience never even enters your mind.

I will never forget what it was like to pull up to West Desoto Street in Pensacola. The church was beautiful, but that's not what got my attention. It was March, and it was about thirty degrees outside and very windy. I was so surprised to find that people had lined up outside to go to church! I had certainly never seen anything like that before. And much like the neighborhood around our church in Augusta, the Brownsville neighborhood was not a place where people would be wanting to line up outside. But there they were! Even as we pulled up into the parking lot, I could feel God in a way I'd never felt Him before.

When we walked into the sanctuary and found a seat, I wish I could fully describe to you what I began to feel. First of all, walking into the sanctuary and finding a seat was quite a problem, because hundreds of people were rushing in to do exactly the same thing. I'm told that Brownsville could seat somewhere around 2,400 people, and during the revival, it usually filled to capacity in about sixty seconds.

As we found a place to sit, the air around us just felt so heavy. It wasn't scary, really, but it was just so completely different from anything I had ever felt before. It was like trying to breathe underwater, the air was so heavy. I was only eleven years old, so I did not know that the Hebrew word for glory is *kabod*, the heavy, weighty presence of the Lord. I could not have told you that, but I absolutely experienced it. It felt like the air was so thick I could have cut it with a knife. I experienced *kabod*, God's glory!

I remember that the worship time lasted for about two and a half hours. At our church, a normal worship time would have lasted for about twenty-five minutes, maybe longer if God was really moving. But people all over Brownsville were totally engaged with the Lord, and they did not even seem to think that worship was going long. I had never heard any of the songs before, but they were mostly just simple love songs to Jesus.

Pastor John Kilpatrick came to the pulpit. I fully expected him to end the service since worship had gone for so long. But that is not at all what happened. He looked at his watch and said, "I'll tell you what we're going to do: we're going to take about a ten-minute break, and then we'll come right back into the service." I was shocked! How long was this thing going to go on, anyway? And who takes an intermission in the middle of a meeting?

My little brother, Philip, was about eight years old. He was getting tired and he needed a snack. A nice lady from Brownsville took Mom to where she could get him some crackers and a drink, and the service started back up about fifteen minutes later. The next thing I knew, here came Steve Hill.

Evangelist Steve Hill preached the Gospel like no one I had ever heard before. It wasn't a sermon; it was an ultimatum! He preached like it was an emergency. He was saying things like this: "You can go to hell wearing a choir robe! You can go to hell with baptismal waters dripping down your face. You can go to hell holding a cup of communion juice. Friend, you have to get right with God! Religion is hanging around the Cross; Christianity is getting on the Cross!"

I felt such heavy conviction in the room. I've often said that the way Steve preached made me want to repent of things I had never even done. That's just how it felt. The convicting power of the Holy Spirit at Brownsville was something I have seldom felt anywhere else.

When Evangelist Steve had finished preaching, he gave an altar call. I had only ever seen a few people get saved at a time in my entire life, but that night at Brownsville, somewhere around 1,000 people literally ran to the altar to give their lives to Jesus

Christ. It was breathtaking, to say the least. I asked myself for the thousandth time, "What is going on in this church?"

After the salvation altar call, Steve invited all the first-time guests down to the altar, saying that he and Pastor Kilpatrick and the Brownsville prayer team wanted to pray for God to give us all a fresh touch of the Holy Spirit. By now, the service had been going on for around four and a half hours. I was tired, and Philip was just done. Mom told my dad, "I'll just stay back here with the kids, and that way you can go get prayer."

Dad took three steps down the aisle, but he spun around on his heel and said, "No! We came as a family; we're getting prayer as a family." Those were the words that caused our whole lives to be completely transformed. Three steps and a declaration made all the difference in the world.

The four of us walked down to the altar call. We were at the very back, because no one else apparently had to think about whether they wanted God to touch them. No one at Brownsville even knew our family. Pastor Kilpatrick knew Granddaddy, but as he wasn't with us and Pastor didn't know the rest of the family, we were totally anonymous in that room. I was standing in front of Dad, and Philip was standing in front of Mom.

Steve was giving some housekeeping instructions. He was telling everyone, "Don't let anyone pray for you unless they have a prayer team badge." It was purely instructional. He was not even looking in our direction. There was no way we could have anticipated what was about to happen to us.

Suddenly, right out of nowhere, he spun around and pointed at Dad, shouting, "Sir! The anointing is raining all over you and your family!"

Dad kind of mildly said, "Okay." I was horrified. Now the crazy man was yelling at us! But I could feel God's presence so strongly in that altar.

Steve tried to continue with his instructions, but he just couldn't. He pointed to us again, and shouted, "No, I said it's raining all over you!" At that moment, he came flying off the platform toward us. I was the first person in my family whom he prayed for. He took my face in his hands and said, "Sis, the anointing is all over you, and it's what is going to carry you through."

When he spoke those words over my life, the Holy Spirit came upon me in a strength that I have no vocabulary for. I did not take a "courtesy fall." My legs were simply swept out from under me. I went down under the power of God, and I'm not talking about a little five-minute interval. If anything, I wanted to get up. That weighty presence of God was all over me, but I fought against it. I strained the muscles in my neck trying to get up. Mom saw me fighting it, so she leaned over and said, "You know, if you'd just let the Lord touch you, you'd feel better." So I let my head rest on that carpet as the Spirit of God surged through me like electricity.

You see, I grew up knowing that I had a call of God on my life. I knew that He had His hand on me to sing, but even though my whole family was musical, I was terrified to sing. I remember hiding behind the pews and shaking. I can remember being in my bedroom as a young girl and telling the Lord, "I know You've called me. I know You have Your hand on my life, but I cannot do this! I can't get up in front of people." But that night, on the floor of Brownsville, God took all that fear right out of my life. I became a whole new person. From that moment until now, I have preached, prophesied, and led worship without fear.

Dad and I were out under the power of God in the altar, but Mom and Philip were still standing. You must understand, my brother was never the kid who made up wild, imaginative stories. He is a very calm person—always has been, always will be. I've often jokingly said that Phil has ice water in his veins. But that night in the altar, he started tugging on Mom's jacket sleeve.

Mom was crying and praying, and God was touching her. She said to Philip, "Not now, son. Mama is praying."

A couple of minutes went by, and he started tugging on her sleeve again—this time, more forcefully. "Mama! Mama!"

With less patience in her voice, she said, "Son, I'm trying to pray."

A couple more minutes went by, but he pulled on her sleeve yet again and said, "Mama!"

Mom said, "What?"

Philip said, "Mama, there is this golden rain falling all around us, all over this room. And Jesus is standing right over there, and He is smiling and waving at us. What's going on in this church?"

And Mom said with tears, "I don't know!"

You see, what was happening was revival. It was deep. It was the kind of move of God that was saving people, healing people, breaking off generational curses, and launching people into their calling. This was not some series of extended meetings. This was a head-on collision with the Spirit of God. What happened to the Stanley family that night in March of 1996 left us forever branded by the Holy Spirit. We have never found a way to be normal since then.

When we went home to our church that Sunday, we were so terrified to tell everyone what had happened to us, because we just knew they'd run us out of the church. Great people of faith that we were, we just didn't say anything at all. Mom and Dad led worship, and I was on the drums. We were at the 8:30 service, which was usually dry and boring. But that Sunday morning, something was noticeably different for us. We could feel God's presence in the room. Dad went to transition the service, and he simply said, "If anyone wants prayer this morning, we are just going to pray that God would give you a fresh touch of His Spirit. Come down to the front."

I had a bird's-eye view of what happened next, because I was playing the drums that morning. I watched as a precious couple in the church, Bill and Mary Thomas, came to the front holding hands. We had no catchers or anything, because none of us actually thought God was going to do anything. I remember Dad barely touched Bill's forehead and said, "Father, in the name of Jesus…." I don't think Dad ever got another word out. Bill reacted as though someone had bashed him in the head with a baseball bat. Down he went, and he took Mary out with him! They were laughing and being wrecked by the Holy Spirit, and Dad was so shocked that God had shown up, he didn't know what to do at first.

He didn't have to think about it for long, because the power of God was unleashed in that early service. The whole sanctuary became the scene of holy pandemonium as God's presence began to sweep over the room. The 8:30 service quickly rolled over into the 11:00 service, and it was clear that something powerful was happening. This was not even close to church as usual. The altar was full of people who were repenting and being touched by God. First one person and then another came up to us and asked, "What in the world happened to y'all?!"

Dad smiled and said, "You know, it would be easier if we just showed you."

We fired up the old church van and just started busing people down to Pensacola every week. In a matter of a few weeks, our church was turned upside down by the Holy Spirit! It was almost funny, because all the people who had been pretending to get saved actually got saved and testified to that fact. Lives were being restored. Marriages were being rekindled. Addictions that had held on to people for years were being broken. Lives were being set on fire for Jesus. It was good, old-fashioned revival, and it was changing everyone it touched!

I thank God all the time that He got ahold of my life right before my twelfth birthday. He caught me early in my life, and He marked me so deeply that I could never be satisfied with less than the reality of His presence. If I could take you to Georgia right now, I would be able to introduce you to people who are still on fire, still free, and still in love with Jesus because of what happened to us in 1996. You see, revival wasn't a cliché to us anymore. It had become more real to us than the air that we breathed.

I also had the privilege of being the worship leader of the Bay Revival that broke out at Church of His Presence in Daphne, Alabama, also under the leadership of Pastor John Kilpatrick. The Bay Revival continued for about two and a half years, and we saw thousands of people meet Jesus Christ, get delivered, and receive their healing. God TV chose to broadcast that move of God to the nations of the world, so there is no way to measure all that God did on this side of eternity. I remember receiving emails from people all over the world, testifying that they had been saved and healed just by watching online.

To this day, I'm amazed that God would allow me to be a witness to major moves of His Spirit, and I am humbled beyond words that I even had a reserved seat, let alone a responsibility to serve. All I can say is that God's goodness and willingness to meet with His people cannot possibly be exaggerated. He is so good!

As you have heard a little bit about my journey into revival, I want you to know that I understand why some people hesitate to use the word *revival*. After all, especially in the United States, we have seen so many misuses of that word that it can leave a bad taste in your mouth. Having grown up going to the Brownsville Revival and having been a part of the leadership at the Bay Revival, my heart is grieved when I hear people use this term in a flippant way to promote their ministry. I want something real, something authentic, something that is birthed by the Spirit of God and finds its roots in the Word of God, or I don't want anything at all.

I am going to give you my personal definition of revival, but before I tell you what it is, let me tell you what it is not. Revival is not good meetings, although I certainly prefer good meetings to bad ones. Revival is not extended meetings or having a special speaker at your church. Revival is not when your service gets a lot of views on YouTube or on Facebook Live. It's not about physical manifestations, even though they do occur and I'm not ashamed of them. It's not about a preacher, a worship leader, or a ministry. None of those things can be defined as revival because they cannot be sustained.

We must have a definition of revival that comes from the Word of God. That is necessary because we are looking for a move that is Heaven-sent and Holy Spirit-sustained. We are looking for the invasion of Heaven upon our lives, sustained by prayer and reverence for God.

To reach my definition, I've got to take you with me to London for just a moment. You know, before I married Nathan Marrow, I had always wanted to go to the United Kingdom. Who doesn't love a good British accent? I love that accent so much that I married it! When the Lord brought me and Nathan together, I didn't realize how much time I would end up spending in the UK. I have had the privilege of speaking all over the British Isles, which is not bad for a girl from Georgia. I have such a love for the British people, and I always enjoy spending time across the pond.

On one occasion, we had the opportunity to do a bit of sight-seeing in London. The taxis were expensive, so Nathan decided that we would use the Underground, or the Tube. I'm so glad that he is good with directions, because if I were left to myself, I think I would still be lost somewhere underneath London.

We were standing on the platform and waiting for the train to come. When it pulled up in front of us and the doors opened, an electronic voice called out, "Please mind the gap between the train and the platform." That quote hit me in my spirit, and then I realized what God was speaking to me. This was the definition of revival. God wanted to close the gap!

You see, friend, revival occurs when God shows up by His Spirit to close the gap between our daily experience and what we see demonstrated in the book of Acts. The book of Acts was not the greatest hits album of the Early Church. It was not the highlight reel. What we read about in the twenty-eight chapters of Acts was the normal, average, everyday expectation of everyone who called upon the name of Jesus! When real revival comes, suddenly we find ourselves walking in the fullness of what the Early Church walked in. *Revival is nothing less than a call back to what the Early Church experienced in the book of Acts.*

I don't know about you, friend, but I believe that it is time for us to mind the gap! We must cry out to God until He closes the gap between our daily lives and the book of Acts. It has been a while in the Western world since we have seen believers walking in the reality of authentic revival. It is time for us to understand that without a drastic recalibration in the Body of Christ, we will be nothing more than another ridiculous social club, having a form of godliness but denying the power of God.

Revival is the promise, the inheritance, and even the very identity of the Church. Every time we settle for less, we dilute the potency of what God intended His Church to look like. When we decide that we can make do with what we can produce in our own strength, we are telling the Holy Spirit that we can do church without Him. God, have mercy!

I believe God is raising up a generation of people who are called to be a holy provocation—to provoke the Church toward revival and the lost toward repentance. God is calling remnant ministers to burn with a passion for Holy Ghost outpouring, who will not stop until the Church is a glorious bride, without spot or wrinkle. God is restoring the Church to its original, on-fire, revival identity!

I remember when my oldest son, Malachi, was born. As rookie parents, Nathan and I were just caught up in the awe of having just brought a little life into the world. It felt like so much was happening all around us, and we had no idea what to expect next. But I was intrigued to find out that it took very little time for the hospital administrative team to send someone in with paperwork. Why? It's because it is always vitally important to put a name on what has been birthed.

On the Day of Pentecost, in Acts chapter 2, Peter stood up in front of the people who had gathered and made an announcement that rocked everyone standing there. I believe that Peter was not just trying to preach a sermon. He was making a birth announcement! He was saying, "Let me tell you what the baby's name is! What has just been birthed is called 'Outpouring!'"

> *But Peter, taking his stand with the eleven, raised his voice and declared to them: "Men of Judea and all you who live in Jerusalem, let this be known to you and give heed to my words. For these men are not drunk, as you suppose, for it is only the third hour of the day; but this is what was spoken of through the prophet Joel:*
>
> *"'And it shall be in the last days,' God says, 'that I will pour forth of My Spirit on all mankind; and your sons and your daughters shall prophesy, and your young men shall see visions, and your old men shall dream dreams; even on My bondslaves, both*

> *men and women, I will in those days pour forth of My Spirit and they shall prophesy*'" (Acts 2:14-18).

I want you to notice that in an outpouring, there is no gender gap, because Peter said that both the sons and the daughters would prophesy. No one cared who received the attention. No one needed special groups to convince people that Jesus was a good idea. I'm not necessarily against having a special group, but in a real revival, no one cares whether or not the men go fishing and the women go shopping together. It's just all about Jesus!

There is no age gap in revival, because Peter said that the old men would dream dreams and the young men would see visions. In a real move of God, demographics become irrelevant as all eyes look to Jesus and begin to encounter Him by His Spirit. What if the solution to the problem of racism is actually an old-fashioned Holy Ghost revival? What if the kids don't want to go to kids' church because they're so caught up in the glory of the Lord? What if the youth group and the young adults are hit by the power of God, and they stop caring about pizza nights or video games? In a real outpouring, every age and demographic is swept up in the mighty flow of the river of God, and everyone becomes supremely fascinated with Jesus Christ.

When we read the historical account of the Early Church and think that they experienced something exceptional, we unintentionally deny the power of the Holy Spirit that is still available to us today. Luke wrote the book of Acts as a matter of fact, historical report on what the Early Church was and how they lived. This was normal life among the believers. We think, "Oh, wow! Peter's shadow healed the sick!" But for the Early Church, this was just another normal experience for a group of people who had met the Messiah and been empowered by His Spirit.

Friend, it's time for us to mind the gap! God, have mercy on us for settling for so much less than what You purchased with the blood of Your Son!

The Early Church had no sense at all of a need to please the people around them. They had no need to be popular. None of them had ever even used the word *relevant*. When they received the power of the Holy Spirit, they were gloriously set free from the opinions of people. They just burned with Holy Ghost power until everyone around them had to decide for or against Jesus Christ.

Let me ask you this: when was the last time someone came under the conviction of the Holy Spirit simply because you walked into the room? Is your life a holy provocation? Does your life make somebody want to know Jesus more, or do you bow to popular opinion?

The leadership of the Early Church had councils that would come together and make unilateral decisions for the Body of Christ. These were men of faith and power, men of prayer and wisdom. Those councils had far-reaching effects on the Church, but I have noticed that none of them ever met to discuss how they could make the message of the Cross more appealing to outsiders. None of them were trying to see how worldly they could live so they could reach out to people around them. They were not trying to make lost people comfortable by compromising. No—they lived in radical holiness, they preached the uncompromising truth of Jesus Christ, and if their message made people uncomfortable, that was just too bad. The apostle Paul even went on to make it quite clear that we should expect the message of the Cross to be offensive. It comes with the package! In Galatians 1:10, Paul said:

> *For am I now seeking the favor of men, or of God? Or am I striving to please men? If I were still trying to please men, I would not be a bond-servant of Christ.*

When I was a little girl, I never dreamed that I would grow up to see my nation in such a backslidden condition of depravity. I expect the world to act like the world, but surely it's not too much to expect the Church to act like the Church! Especially in Western society, we have people who claim to know Jesus, yet they are "not sure" if He is the only way to God. They are "not sure" that the Bible is the infallible Word of God. They are "not sure" if healing and deliverance are for today. They are "not sure" what to believe about sexuality.

My friend, when we become willing to sell the truth off at auction to keep from offending the world around us or to keep the big givers happy, it is time to mind the gap! When we would rather avoid bad press than take a stand for the truth of the Word of God, it is an indication that we are not serving Jesus and His Spirit is not among us. The Holy Spirit bears witness to the Word, testifying of Jesus Christ! In real revival, we believe the Book and we live out what it says, no matter what anyone thinks and no matter the cost.

As my husband and I travel throughout the USA, people often ask us, "Was the church you just ministered in an on-fire church, or was it a religious church?" In the book of Acts, there was no such distinction. There was no "religious church" or "on-fire church." You were burning for Jesus or you simply were not saved. There was no middle ground.

None of these people had to be encouraged to be passionate about Jesus. They had experienced Him; they had walked with Him and talked with Him, and there was no turning back. Their passion did not come from a place of hype or from attending a popular conference. It came from an encounter with the King, and they had become addicted to the sound of His voice.

The reason we make a distinction between religious churches and on-fire churches today is simply because the Western world has produced so many false converts. We have preached a people-pleasing, seeker-sensitive gospel, so we have people mentally agreeing with an idea about Jesus, but they have not been changed. We try to get people to make a decision for Jesus, but the Early Church saw people transferred from the kingdom of darkness into the Kingdom of God.

What the Early Church had was Good News, but it was also offensive to the flesh. When people got saved in the Early Church, they were not just latching on to a new intellectual idea; they were being radically transformed by God's Spirit! And they didn't have fakers, either. They had run into the living, breathing Son of God, and they could not be talked out of their experience. The Early Church preached their Gospel all the way to the chopping blocks where they lost their heads, to the stakes they were burned on, to the crosses they were nailed to, and everything else the enemy used to try to silence them.

If you want to know whether you've become a people pleaser, ask yourself this: would I live and die for the messages that I'm hearing and preaching? Am I only being blessed or am I being challenged? Am I being taught the Word of God, or is this preacher just popular on YouTube? Could I stand up for this message with my dying breath?

In the book of Acts, there was no such thing as a powerless Christian. You were walking in the *dunamis,* power, of the Holy Spirit, or you simply did not know Jesus. In our day, we go to great lengths to make up new theology to excuse our lack of power. People preach that miracles are not for today, but it is usually because they have never prayed through to see a miracle for themselves. If we prayed like the Early Church prayed, we would see what they saw in our midst. We must start believing and praying in faith until our experience lines up with God's Word.

I do not have the right to base what I believe on my own experience. Everything I believe must have its foundation in the unchanging, eternal Word of God. That means that I must press in for miracles because they are all over the Bible, and when I do, my experience soon lines up with my belief. Powerlessness in the Church is an evil thing, and we cannot condone it or pretend that it's normal. We have to stop accusing God of doing nothing when we have not yet begun to pray. We must mind the gap!

I want us to look at a prayer from the Psalms that is both a repentance and revival prayer all at the same time. In fact, we see in this prayer that repentance and revival are biblically inseparable. Psalm 85:4-9 says:

> *Restore us, O God of our salvation, and cause Your indignation toward us to cease. Will You be angry with us forever? Will You prolong Your anger to all generations? Will You not Yourself revive us again,*

> *that Your people may rejoice in You? Show us Your lovingkindness, O Lord, and grant us Your salvation. I will hear what God the Lord will say; for He will speak peace to His people, to His godly ones; but let them not turn back to folly. Surely His salvation is near to those who fear Him, that glory may dwell in our land.*

God wants His glory to settle down, to dwell among His people, which is the ultimate expression of revival. He wants everything that was happening in the Early Church to be manifested in fullness today. He wants to reveal the glory of Jesus through our lives.

When God makes Himself at home among His people, we will see the culture around us bow to the mighty name of Jesus. In every historical revival, we see God coming to His people and allowing His presence to abide in great intensity, with great signs and wonders following those who believe. Entire regions and nations have come under the glory of God. Surely, this is revival. Oh, God, do it again!

For God to dwell in us, we must prepare our lives to be His temple. This is why Paul said to the Church, "Don't you know that your body is the Temple of the Holy Spirit?" (See 1 Corinthians 6:19.) God is looking for our lives to once again become the sanctified space in which His glory can dwell. For God to come in revival and glory, we must learn again what it means to walk as consecrated people who love holiness and God's presence more than we love to be stroked and entertained.

I have taken the liberty of making a list of things that were considered to be normal to the Early Church according to the book of Acts. This list is by no means exhaustive, but you may find it to be a good place to start in our study. This list has become a prayer list for me and my family, because every time we see revival reality in the pages of the book of Acts, it makes us cry out for more of God. Let it cause you to do the same, and please feel free to add to this list.

NORMAL EXPERIENCES IN THE BOOK OF ACTS

- They healed the sick without exception. We have no record of anyone in Acts coming to the Church and not receiving their healing. What if we had the audacity to go ahead and pray for the sick? People ask all the time, "What if they don't get healed?" Friend, what if they do? I promise you—you will not see healing unless you step out in faith and pray for the sick. We must trust that our God is Jehovah Rapha, the Lord our Healer, and He has not changed. He still heals today.
- They cast out devils. They didn't make a big deal about it, either. They were not ashamed to deal with deliverance, and they didn't make it a show; they just did it.
- They spoke truth to power, even when they knew that it would send them to jail or to their death. Nothing demonstrates this boldness quite like Acts 4, when the religious authorities threatened Peter and John, commanding them to no longer speak in the name of Jesus. Without hesitation, Peter and John told them

that they could not help but preach what they had seen or heard, even though they knew it could cost them everything. Instead of bowing to that religious spirit, they prayed that God would fill them with boldness to speak His Word, confirming it with signs and wonders.

- They demonstrated extreme generosity (see Acts 5). The Church in Jerusalem "had all things in common." People have used that phrase to say that the Early Church practiced a form of socialism; that is simply not the case. It was not a system of governing; it was an offering that got out of control. The believers in Jerusalem believed the prophecy of Jesus that Jerusalem would be destroyed; they knew they couldn't hold on to their property. When needs would arise, people simply sold their property to make sure their brothers and sisters in Christ would have their needs met. This wasn't done under compulsion; it was a spirit of generosity. Every authentic move of God from then until now has shown the same generous spirit. For instance, the wonderful, predominately low-income people of the Azusa Street Revival funded missionaries around the world.
- The Early Church forgave and even prayed for their persecutors, winning some of them to Christ (see Acts 16).

- They frequently called spontaneous prayer meetings that had 100 percent attendance. In our day, the prayer meeting is usually the least attended meeting, but prayer was the life source of the Early Church.
- Their first reaction to opposition was always prayer.
- They raised the dead. This one bothers us today, because we have not seen much of this in modern times. That does not excuse us from pressing in. The Jesus we serve said that He is the Resurrection and the Life. In the book of Acts, we see both Peter and Paul raise the dead, neither of them treating that miracle as though it were superior to any other kind of miracle.
- They took every opportunity to spread the Gospel. Normal believers did this, not just the apostles.
- They frequently heard the voice of God. Sometimes He spoke to them in visions, dreams, trances, or directly to their spirit. They did not go around trying to find someone else to get a word from God for them; rather, they prayed until they heard Him for themselves. Jesus tells us in John 10:27 that His sheep hear His voice, and the Early Church certainly demonstrated that. I thank God for the fivefold gift of the prophet and I know several prophets,

> but I thank God that He speaks to me because I am His child.

Just as I had a head-on collision with Holy Spirit in March of 1996, just like the Early Church had one in the second chapter of Acts, and just like God has done at various points in history, God would like to invade the nations of the world once again. We need an international great awakening that will change legislation, transform societies, and cause the name of Jesus Christ to be magnified once again. We need a Holy Ghost revival that will bring millions, even billions of people to the Lord.

At the time of this writing, we are seeing certain nations line up in a posture of war. It feels like we are entering a pivotal time in history. I believe that these are the last of the last days. To be honest, it would be easy to turn on the news and feel afraid and uncertain. When we see major world powers aligning with what we see in biblical eschatology, it can make our hearts feel weighed down with anxiety.

I hope you will hear my heart in this: while I am concerned for the victims of these "wars and rumors of wars," while I contend for them in prayer, my heart is filled with joy. Why? It is because revival has never occurred when the conditions were good. Revival has always occurred when it seemed as though all hope was lost. In church history, we see that the worst of times have really been the best of times.

It may seem darker than usual on the world scene right now, but, my brother or sister, this is a season for us to lift up our eyes to King Jesus and cry out for Him to pour out His Spirit once again! He is famous for baptizing His people in the Holy Spirit and with fire. I know firsthand that He will come if we invite Him to.

Invite Him to come to your house first, and then let's cry out for Him to come to our churches once again. May the God of the book of Acts make Himself obvious in this season!

As we begin this journey together, I dare you to pray this prayer with me:

> *Father, in the name of Jesus, I ask you to set my life on fire with the holy flames of revival. I want to experience what the Early Church did. I want the fire of Pentecost to overwhelm my life, and I will not settle for less than the outpouring of Your Spirit in my life. In Jesus' name, amen.*

Chapter 2

LOOKING FOR A LADDER

He had a dream, and behold, a ladder was set on the earth with its top reaching to heaven; and behold, the angels of God were ascending and descending on it. And behold, the Lord stood above it and said, "I am the Lord, the God of your father Abraham and the God of Isaac; the land on which you lie, I will give it to you and to your descendants" (Genesis 28:12-13).

AT THIRTY-EIGHT YEARS OLD, I'm happy to say that most people will still say that I am relatively young, though I may or may not be covering up some gray hair. I like to think of it as fighting the good fight. I am not yet old, but I am not exactly young, either. And because of the way God has orchestrated my life, I have had some amazing experiences, both in the United States and in many other nations.

By God's great grace, I have had the privilege to minister in other parts of the world on platforms that I'm sure I did not belong on. I have gotten to be a part of so many wonderful ministry moments when the Body of Christ came together in such a way that it took my breath. I can truly say that God has been good to me.

I have had some wonderful experiences in my personal life. I can trace the hand of God and His goodness throughout my journey, and the moments He has given me have been so wonderful. I think of experiencing revival, both at Brownsville and at the Bay. I recall moving to Daphne, Alabama, to serve as the worship pastor for Pastor John Kilpatrick at Church of His Presence. I remember the joy of marrying my husband, Nathan Marrow, and how deliriously happy we were on our wedding day. I love the moments that some people would call ordinary, like just having coffee together with Nathan, enjoying each other's company.

I have experienced both joy and strength, and I have seen great loss and sorrow. But let me tell you this: nothing, and I do mean nothing, has ever come close to what it felt like to bring life into the world.

Nathan and I have two little boys. Malachi David was born in 2016 and Jeremiah Nathan was born in 2018. Everyone tells you that when you have kids, they will get a hold of your heart in a way that nothing else ever could. The hype is definitely true! It was love at first sight with both of our little men. I will never forget hearing those tiny voices for the first time. I remember looking into those big blue eyes. I remember holding them close and realizing that God had entrusted them to us. Man, I was a goner!

I used to live my life and minister for the sake of the call God had given to me personally. Nothing deeper had ever really occurred to me. But the day I became a mother, I had a whole new reason. There is nothing like having kids to show you that your life and the way you live it is not just for your own sake; another generation is depending on my obedience to Jesus Christ. Two little boys will one day be two grown men, and it is my job to make sure that they know Jesus, that they know the power of prayer, and that they know how to live a life of holiness. This stopped being about Nathan and me a long time ago. We are living this life for the next generation!

As I look at the United States in this particular moment of history, I cannot help but see how self-absorbed we have become. Our society has become so narcissistic, and so have our policies. Believe me when I tell you, this selfishness has corrupted all aspects of the political system, and we can't afford to act like the Church is any better. Our decisions, our beliefs, our expressions, and our ministries have begun to reflect this thought: *I am in this thing for my own sake.* We would never say it that way, but if we honestly allow the Holy Spirit to convict us in light of God's Word, most of us are living for the present moment. My concern is that the next generation stands to reap what we are sowing right now.

I am asking God to wake us up to the fact that what we invest our lives in today will be the harvest that the next generation will reap. The way I live in this moment is directly affecting my boys and, if Jesus tarries, their children after them. We are all connected in a beautiful chain of grace, and we must press in for the sake of the next generation!

Friend, please allow this to sound an alarm in your spirit! Look at the way the so-called people of God are living right now. Look at how we talk to each other, both in person and through social media. We can see the evidence of selfish ambition and arrogance within our churches. In many cases, we would be hard-pressed to discover a difference between us and the world we have been called to reach. People in the Church are covering up addiction. People in the Church are cheating on their spouses. People in the Church are stealing money. The list could go on, but I want you to realize that every one of those sins will touch more than just a single life. Our choices reverberate to our children.

Are we going to leave a legacy of trying to see what we can get away with, or are we actually going to live for God with all that we have? Are we going to demonstrate hope and holiness and hunger for God's righteousness, or are we going to demonstrate apathy and indifference to the moral decay all around us? Are we going to pretend that nothing is wrong, or are we going to cry out to God for mercy and outpouring? What is it going to take to provoke the people of God to return to the altar of prayer?

At this point in my own life, I look behind me to my own history and heritage. I have always loved my family, and I was raised to appreciate their voices in my life, but the longer I live the more aware I am that I owe a massive debt of gratitude to my "Abraham Generation."

In the last chapter, I spoke briefly about my granddaddy's influence in my life. It would be difficult to overestimate the impact he made on my heart. John Moore paid an incredible price in his life and in his ministry to see God use his family for the Kingdom. In fact, he cared more about empowering his family to do what God called us to than he did about his own ministry opportunities.

When God called me to lead worship, Granddaddy gave me the upright piano that had been in my grandparents' house for years. When Granddaddy realized that I was called to preach, he put me to work right away. I'm not even sure if that was a good idea; in fact, I cringe on the inside when I think of those formative messages I preached. I'm so grateful that live streaming had not yet been invented to document every baby step of my learning experience. But it did not bother him at all. He trusted me with his pulpit when I could not have been mature enough to deserve that trust.

I would preach a message, and then he would invite me over to his house. He would fix me a ham and cheese omelet, brew a nice cup of coffee, and sit down to talk about my message. If I had done well, he would chuckle and say, "Well, honey, hold on to those notes. If it preached good once, it will preach good twice. Matter of fact, I believe I'll steal it and preach it like it ought to be preached!" He would laugh that big, booming laugh, and I would feel like a million bucks because I had made my Granddaddy proud.

There were other times that he would sit me down with that omelet and say, "Young lady, do you remember when you said so and so in your message? Don't ever say that again. If you can't prove something with two or three scriptures, you have no business preaching it from the pulpit. We're not called to preach our opinions; we are called to preach the Word of God." I don't know if you're aware of it or not, but that is real mentoring. That is speaking the truth in love, and we need so much more of this.

He lived out what it meant to walk with God while we all watched in wonder. He was far from perfect; he had his weaknesses. But I watched his life. John Moore was one of those "once in a lifetime" people, the kind of man whose life really matched his message. He was the kind of man who preached holiness and practiced compassion. He mentored our family in ministry, instilling in us a desire for integrity and the reality of God's presence. He was my Abraham.

I have watched Mom and Dad and their generation in our family carry on the way Granddaddy taught us to. None of them would dare to claim perfection or anything close to it; however, they knew who to run to when they had fallen short. Granddaddy taught them to run to Jesus, and that is exactly what they did. I'm so glad they did, because my brother and I were watching.

Mom and Dad were the Isaac Generation. They carried on. They did the hard work. Just like Isaac in the Bible, they dug wells of revival and held on to what Granddaddy, our Abraham, had taught us. I remember watching them go through pain and betrayal in ministry that would certainly have taken out lesser people. I saw the tears they didn't think I saw. I heard the pain in their voices. I heard them praying when they didn't know I was in the room. I heard them take their tears to Jesus, and that made all the difference. I learned that there is no way to avoid being hurt, but you can absolutely decide where you're going to take that pain. I learned how to forgive by their example. I learned who to lean on by watching the Isaac Generation.

But there comes a time when Jacob has to set out on his own, and he has to hear from God for himself. In my life, I am very aware that the mantle of John Moore is resting upon my family, and what we do with it will make all the difference for the generation that comes behind us. I don't want to waste the mantle of a great man of God. I don't want to take the richness of my spiritual heritage for granted. I don't want to cause the next generation to suffer loss because of my spiritual laziness and apathy.

In Genesis 28, Jacob has come to a painful reality about himself. He is just realizing that his deceitful scheming has caused him to lose his immediate family. If you examine Jacob's life story in Scripture, you will find that he never again saw his mother and father alive. The man who always had an angle was finally realizing that he had gambled and lost it all.

Striving and seeking for position and power was causing Jacob to lose out on everything that he thought was so precious. It is a serious thing when a grown man runs away from home, but that is what happened to Jacob. All that scheming to steal Esau's birthright, and all Jacob had to show for it was a one-way ticket to Uncle Laban's house.

You see, the Jacob Generation is made up of people who will not settle for doctrine only. They're not going to take your word for anything. The Jacob Generation requires an actual encounter with the God of Abraham and Isaac. They need their own experience, because what happened in years gone by means next to nothing to them.

When my family and my church found themselves bound in religion, I had to have an encounter in my own life. Even though I was young, I had been raised to know what I believed. I could quote Scriptures left and right, and I could even quote statements of faith from our denomination. I had heard stories from my parents and grandparents about moments they'd had with God. But I also knew that something was terribly wrong with the way we were doing church. It simply was not enough. Worse than that, it was boring.

The reason the Millennials and Gen Z are struggling with our statements of faith is because our lives have not matched our message. It's going to take more than good preaching for these people; they want a Jesus they can experience for themselves. Talking about God is not sufficient. They want God to be demonstrated to them in their daily life, and who can blame them? In the words of the famous theologian Elvis Presley, "A little less conversation, a little more action," please. Talk is cheap. What the destitute Jacob needs is an encounter.

The good news is this: God has a ladder for every runaway Jacob! God knows how to set Jacob up for an encounter that will leave him irrevocably changed.

I want us to take a look at Genesis 28:10-22.

> *Then Jacob departed from Beersheba and went toward Haran. He came to a certain place and spent the night there, because the sun had set; and he took one of the stones of the place and put it under his*

head, and lay down in that place. He had a dream, and behold, a ladder was set on the earth with its top reaching to heaven; and behold, the angels of God were ascending and descending on it. And behold, the Lord stood above it and said, "I am the Lord, the God of your father Abraham and the God of Isaac; the land on which you lie, I will give it to you and to your descendants. Your descendants will also be like the dust of the earth, and you will spread out to the west and to the east and to the north and to the south; and in you and in your descendants shall all the families of the earth be blessed. Behold, I am with you and will keep you wherever you go, and will bring you back to this land; for I will not leave you until I have done what I have promised you." Then Jacob awoke from his sleep and said, "Surely the Lord is in this place, and I did not know it." He was afraid and said, "How awesome is this place! This is none other than the house of God, and this is the gate of heaven."

So Jacob rose early in the morning, and took the stone that he had put under his head and set it up as a pillar and poured oil on its top. He called the name of that place Bethel; however, previously the name of the city had been Luz. Then Jacob made a vow, saying, "If God will be with me and will keep me on this journey that I take, and will give me food to eat and garments to wear, and I return to my father's house in safety, then the Lord will be my God. This stone, which I have set up as a pillar, will be God's

> *house, and of all that You give me I will surely give a tenth to You."*

Until this moment of encounter, Jacob had no concept of serving anyone other than himself and his own purposes. He was his own god, the center of his own world. Jacob felt entitled. He was famous for using people to get what he wanted. But one moment of encounter caused him to say, "Now, You are not just Abraham's God. You are not just Isaac's God. Now, I claim You for myself. If You really are who You say You are, You can have my whole life." This is the surrender of a man who was done fighting, done making excuses. One encounter is all it takes.

Friend, you can always tell who is a part of the Jacob Generation, because they are the ones who will give God all that they are if they find Him to be real. They may have a rough exterior, but on the inside they are desperate to know if the God of their grandfather is real and is interested in them. The experience of their parents will not suffice for them. Our flashy lights and church showmanship will not suffice for them. They are not looking for a show that has been well-produced; they are looking for the ladder that will connect their life to another realm—the realm of eternity!

The Jacob Generation is only one supernatural encounter away from stepping into their divine purpose. They are one altar call away from picking up where their forefathers left off.

It would be easy as the Abraham or Isaac Generation to be frustrated with the doctrine of this current generation. I often find myself frustrated that no one takes the time to know what they believe. But I am convinced that if we can just get Jacob to the ladder, his experience with God will send shock waves through his belief system, confronting him with the reality of who God is. This generation is longing for something that they have no language for, because regardless of the darkness they are bound with at the moment, God has deposited a craving for eternity within them, and they will be satisfied with nothing less than God Himself.

> *He has also set eternity in their heart, yet so that man will not find out the work which God has done from the beginning even to the end* (Ecclesiastes 3:11).

Now, I understand that Jacob's ladder encounter did not solve all the problems in his life, or even with his spirituality. The man still had a long way to go. I get it. But I want us to understand something powerful about this ladder. What we are about to see is the key to seeing the Jacob Generation experience a life-changing, personal revival.

The ladder is not an object; *it is nothing less than the Person of Jesus Christ!*

> *Jesus saw Nathanael coming to Him, and said of him, "Behold, an Israelite indeed, in whom there is no deceit!" Nathanael said to Him, "How do You know me?" Jesus answered and said to him, "Before Philip called you, when you were under the fig tree, I saw you." Nathanael answered Him, "Rabbi, You are the Son of God; You are the King of Israel." Jesus answered and said to him, "Because I said to you that I saw you under the fig tree, do you believe? You will see greater things than these." And He said to him, "Truly, truly, I say to you, you will see the*

heavens opened and the angels of God ascending and descending on the Son of Man" (John 1:47-51).

The thing about the Jacob Generation is that you will never impress them with your church-marketing strategy. Your ministry promotional video will just go in one ear and out the other, no matter how epic you make the soundtrack. Jacob can recognize a scheme a mile away. But instead of trying to recruit them to your cause, you must introduce them to your friend, the ladder! They need Jesus!

You see, I told you about my Abraham and my Isaac. But to my two little boys, to Malachi and Jeremiah, the cycle starts again. They've never met my granddaddy, but they're watching our lives right now. They have to meet the God of my fathers. They have to know that this Jesus thing is for real. They must understand that this is not something their parents do for a living; they have to have their hearts set on fire by the flames that ignited us!

I have been so blessed beyond measure to have experienced revival at Brownsville and at the Bay Revival. I had landmark moments in both of those revivals that have become defining elements of my walk with God. They are a part of my spiritual DNA, and I can make no apology for that.

But one of the things that those two moves of God have in common is this: they are over. I realize that I carry them within me, but if I were to travel to either of the locations where those revivals were held, there are no revival services happening right now. That means that I cannot take Malachi and Jeremiah into those meetings and say, "Boys, this is what Mama means. This is a revival. This is what I encountered." I can't do that.

The two revivals that I was a part of both came to an end, but more than ever before, I am aware of this fact: *we owe the next generation a move of God!* Friend, maybe you come from an Abraham or Isaac Generation, but let me tell you, it is time for us to live the life and pray the prayers that set Jacob up on a collision course with Jesus Christ the Ladder! We must introduce the Jacob Generation to the God of his fathers. We must show them what it looks like to burn with Holy Ghost fire, to live for eternity, and to walk in outrageous faith. It's up to us to show them what a prayer life looks like.

When Jacob ran into the ladder, it set him up for the next season of his life. Jacob wanted to be successful and make something of himself, but the greatest key to surviving his season at Uncle Laban's house was his family. Jacob was trying to accumulate wealth, but as the heir apparent to Isaac, he was trying to work for what he would one day receive through sonship. Laban cheated Jacob over and over again during that season, because accumulating wealth was not what God had in mind for Jacob; God was building a family through him that would become a nation.

Because Jacob met the God of Bethel who is the Ladder that connects our lives to eternity, Jacob would build a family that God could use to bless the nations of the world. I must point this out, because we cannot expect the Jacob Generation to have the same priorities as the generations that went before them.

We must understand that the battleground of this era is family. The enemy is trying to redefine what he has not been able to destroy. If we take a stand for what the Bible says is right, if we live with integrity, if we love our spouse, if we raise godly children, the world will look upon us as radical revolutionaries. No—we are just the Jacob Generation. And when the Jacob Generation makes the choice to walk in biblical integrity, that is when we see the King of Glory come in!

> *Who may ascend into the hill of the Lord? And who may stand in His holy place? He who has clean hands and a pure heart, who has not lifted up his soul to falsehood and has not sworn deceitfully. He shall receive a blessing from the Lord and righteousness from the God of his salvation. This is the generation of those who seek Him, who seek Your face—even Jacob. Selah.*
>
> *Lift up your heads, O gates, and be lifted up, O ancient doors, that the King of glory may come in! Who is the King of glory? The Lord strong and mighty, the Lord mighty in battle. Lift up your heads, O gates, and lift them up, O ancient doors, that the King of glory may come in! Who is this King of glory? The Lord of hosts, He is the King of glory. Selah* (Psalm 24:3-10).

The most wonderful aspect of authentic revival is when the King of Glory comes and takes His rightful place. May we stand and contend for every Jacob to find the Ladder, so that we might host the King of Glory in our midst!

Pray with me:

> *Father, I ask You in the name of Jesus to help my life point the Jacob Generation to the ladder who is Christ Jesus. Let the prayers I pray today and the decisions I make now affect the next generation,*

making them hungry and thirsty for Your righteousness. Fill them with Your Spirit to overflowing, in Jesus' name, amen.

Chapter 3

REFINING OR REDEFINING?

WHEN I WAS EIGHTEEN years old, I went to the Brownsville Revival School of Ministry in Pensacola, Florida. I felt the leading of the Holy Spirit to receive impartation and education at the same place I had been called to the ministry, so Brownsville was the logical choice for me.

Sitting in those services night after night was such a privilege. Granted, the revival itself was over. Modern historians will tell you that the Brownsville Revival continued from 1995 until 2000, when Evangelist Steve Hill moved on to plant a church in Texas. While the revival was over, God was still moving in the church on a very regular basis. The services were so powerful, and they marked my life. There is something so priceless about studying God but also experiencing Him at the same time. My time at Bible school was soaked in prayer and worship, which made the study come alive. It was in those moments that God started giving me songs. It was in that time that He started cultivating a hunger to study, to learn, and to experience Him in a deeper way. I wanted to do more than read books; I wanted to live the kind of life that God would inhabit.

I spent hours weeping before the Lord on that carpet. I got to speak with men and women who had been a part of the revival and gain their wisdom and perspective from those years. My first year of school was filled with precious moments with the Lord, wonderful teachings from men and women of God, and services that helped to mold who I am in Christ.

But I found myself becoming frustrated with something that was happening. Many of the guest speakers who would come to preach would try to explain why revival had come to Brownsville. I couldn't help but notice, it would always turn out that their reason that revival came had a lot to do with the latest book they were trying to sell. What bothered me is that none of those people had actually been there when the revival broke out, so how could they possibly know why it happened? Don't get me wrong; many of them were wonderful men and women of God, but I could not understand why everyone was trying to redefine revival. As the old saying goes, "If it ain't broke, don't fix it."

Not only have I spoken to people who were there before, during, and after the revival took place, but John Kilpatrick is my pastor. From the testimony of those who were there, the revival broke out on Father's Day of 1995 because Brownsville had been praying for two and a half years. They had laid aside the normal American Sunday night service and turned it into a prayer meeting, and they refused to stop praying until the breakthrough came. That is what brought revival. But when Pastor Kilpatrick made the decision to turn that Sunday night service into a prayer meeting, almost no one thought it was a good idea. Sunday nights were one of the most important services in American Pentecostalism at that time. It was unheard of!

One of the reasons we try to redefine revival and its process is because we do not want to pay the price to host an authentic move of God. If you function in a "book of Acts" outpouring of the Holy Spirit, you may become subject to some "book of Acts" persecution. Throughout history, as God poured out His Spirit, the enemy has poured out persecution, and that still applies to us today. The enemy has no new plays in his playbook. If you are going to press in for revival, prepare to be misunderstood, mocked, and misinterpreted. It comes with the territory!

We want a shortcut to revival, so we go through a thousand prayer tunnels, hoping to "get the anointing" from someone else. I wonder how this makes the Holy Spirit feel. He is ready and willing to mark a generation with the fire of God, and yet we do not follow the clear instructions of God's Word that form the prerequisite for revival. We do not want to repent and we certainly don't want to pray.

> *And My people who are called by My name humble themselves and pray and seek My face and turn from their wicked ways, then I will hear from heaven, will forgive heal their land* (2 Chronicles 7:14).

There really are no shortcuts to revival. There are no impartation lines that can take you there. There are no special speakers who could provide a move of God. While God uses all of those things as tools in His hand, the prerequisites for revival are what they always have been: the repentance and prayer of God's people. Anyone who tries to sell you a shortcut as "deep revelation" is lying to you, and they're probably trying to sell you something.

I can't find anywhere in the New Testament where the Early Church chased the big preachers around to get their anointing. Nobody was chasing a preacher; they were chasing after Jesus! They pressed into God for themselves, and they came out with His anointing on their own lives. That is how they changed their world.

Have you ever really thought about the story of Stephen in the book of Acts? This guy was being used by God to do miracles and signs and wonders. He was preaching, and he was taking on the religious leaders of the day. But here's the thing: he did not start doing that while chasing Peter or John or any of the other apostles. He had met God for Himself. And Stephen, this great martyr of the faith, this man was a waiter! We tend to forget that his main responsibility was serving meals to widows in the Church; yet he had had such an encounter with the fire of God that the religious leaders thought he was one of the leaders of the Church, and they killed him for it.

I love the Scripture in Hebrews that says, "Looking unto *Jesus*, the Author and the Finisher of our faith," because He is the only one we should be looking to. The cry of an authentic revivalist is always, "All eyes on Jesus!"

Let me remind you, what you really need can only be found in Jesus! It can never be found in a man, no matter how great you think he is. Oh, that we would truly come back to the place where this is all about Jesus! This is all for His glory! This is all for His honor, and no one else deserves the focus of our attention.

Revival begins when God's people return to the altar, crying out in repentance and fervent prayer. That's why my prayer focus has shifted. I have been asking God to set off a nuclear bomb of Holy Ghost conviction in the Church of the Western world. How we need a mighty move of repentance in the Body of Christ! In every instance where the Church has humbled themselves enough to repent for their own sins and the sins of their nation, we have seen God demonstrate His power. But when the Church has carried on in arrogance, trying to act like they have it all together, we have seen the spirit of religion given first place as the devil claps his hands in delight.

You say that you don't want to have a religious spirit? Good! The greatest weapon in your arsenal against that foul demon is repentance, because a religious spirit and a humble spirit cannot coexist. It takes humility to acknowledge that our churches are full of sin. It takes a contrite heart to admit that we have engaged in competition against other churches and ministries, to the detriment of the Body of Christ. It takes a softness of heart to realize that we have done much to grieve the Holy Spirit, that we have functioned in the fear of man, that we have become more self-conscious than God-conscious, and that we have auctioned off our moral authority for an offering. But only when we humble ourselves and let the sound of weeping fill the altars of our churches again will we see God pour out His Spirit.

When was the last time you heard the weeping and wailing that comes from godly sorrow? When was the last time your church's altars were full of people wailing and travailing in deep repentance? When were you last gripped with the convicting power of the Holy Spirit?

I believe that our first order of repentance should be to ask God to forgive us for allowing godly sorrow to become so rare in His house. Who has told us that repentance is for other people? My Bible shows that Jesus Christ told five out of seven churches in Asia to repent (see Revelation chapters 1–3). If Jesus can call churches to repentance, why have we decided that we are too wonderful to repent? Repentance does not make us look weak; it makes us strong!

We want to preach about breakthrough and joy, but we don't want to talk about weeping and wailing. We don't want to pray the prayers of repentance that birth souls into the Kingdom. That kind of praying gets messy. It's disruptive. It can even be offensive. It certainly invites ridicule from outsiders. But that kind of repentance is always necessary to those who want to see real revival.

That kind of repentance will always lead you into the revival cry. Praying for revival often looks like tears and sounds like groaning. To the outside observer, praying for revival looks like desperate hysteria. There is nothing dignified about it! But that is the kind of praying that gets God's attention and brings about eternal results. Those are the kind of prayers that reverberate through the halls of Heaven. No one in church history has ever heard of a revival that was not prayed for, because no such revival exists. Every move of God that this world has ever seen, including the one in Acts chapter 2, was birthed by praying saints who had stopped caring what everyone thought of them.

As twenty-first-century Christianity seeks to redefine the word *revival* to mean extended meetings, special speakers, or an emphasis on evangelism, I appeal to you today to be a part of a real revival remnant. I dare you to be hungry enough for a real move of God that you become known as a person of prayer. While most so-called ministers try to become social media influencers, start fasting. Begin to cry out in the secret place. While this generation tries to redefine revival and Christianity, to be a real revivalist you will have to submit yourself to the refining place of prayer. It is from that place that real preaching develops, authentic evangelism occurs, and Holy Ghost miracles begin to flow. That's the place where Heaven-kissed anthems of worship are born and you start making real history with God. Prayers birthed in the secret place put such a desire for God in your heart that holiness will flow out of you. You will begin to actually know the God you talk about.

The place of refining stands opposed to your personal comfort. Allowing the Lord to refine your life in the place of prayer is not going to be a smooth ride to a successful ministry. I promise you, you are going to want to get out of it. You're going to want to ask God to make it stop. You will definitely feel like it's taking too long. Refining will be excruciating to your flesh and detrimental to your carnal desires, but the refining work of the Holy Spirit is essential to the life or church that hungers for revival.

> *"Behold, I am going to send My messenger, and he will clear the way before Me. And the Lord, whom you seek, will suddenly come to His temple; and the messenger of the covenant, in whom you delight, behold, He is coming," says the Lord of hosts. "But who can endure the day of His coming? And who can stand when He appears? For He is like a refiner's fire and like fullers' soap. He will sit as a smelter and purifier of silver, and He will purify the sons of Levi and refine them like gold and silver, so that they may present to the Lord offerings in righteousness. Then the offering of Judah and Jerusalem will be pleasing to the Lord as in the days of old and as in former years"* (Malachi 3:1-4).

The process of refining is such a picture of what God wants to do in our lives. First, the metal, such as silver, is heated until it liquefies. The refiner keeps that heat at an intense level, which causes the dross to begin to rise up. Dross is anything that is not pure silver, any mixture or impurity, and the intensity of the fire causes that mixture to rise to the surface, at which point the refiner scoops it off the top. And that's not where the process ends; the refiner heats the silver up again until even more dross rises to the top. The refiner will repeat the whole process until he can see his own reflection in the liquefied metal.

When God refines us with the fire of His Spirit, there comes an intense purification. There comes an extreme sanctification. The heat gets turned up, and your whole life starts being refined by the Holy Spirit. He removes the impurities. He does a deep cleansing. You see, when you set your heart to be a place where the fire of God can come and stay, when you decide that your life is going to host the fire of God, you can no longer get away with what other people can get away with. Suddenly, you become uncomfortable with certain types of entertainment. You can't go where other people go. You can't have the same conversations. You become more aware of God's holiness than you are of your own need for comfort.

The refining fire of God comes to purify the Church! The last time I checked, the Bible still says that Jesus Christ is coming back for a Bride without spot or wrinkle or any such thing. We had better get ready, because the fire of God is about to fall!

> *Behold, I have refined you, but not as silver; I have tested you in the furnace of affliction. For My own sake, for My own sake, I will act; for how can My name be profaned? And My glory I will not give to another* (Isaiah 48:10-11).

I believe we are coming upon a time when the Lord will not continue to allow His Church to misrepresent Him. Someone once said that revival was when God got sick of being misrepresented, so He showed up to represent Himself. And when He does that, you either fall in line with Him or you get left behind. He will not share His glory with another!

I believe that many people short-circuit the process of God for revival in their lives because they want to skip over the refining process of repentance and prayer. It would be much easier if we could just have a better marketing strategy. So many people have filled their churches with programs and their platforms with flashy "sets" that look like a bad cross between a game show and a nightclub. Our churches have done a great job at selling themselves, but a terrible job at introducing people to Jesus.

We need revival, and we all know it. As we travel across the United States, every church that I visit claims to want revival, and I'm sure many of them are sincere. We have people all over this nation who would love to go to revival meetings, but what we are lacking is people who will commit to revival praying. We need intercessors who have been tried by fire, found faithful in the secret place, and purified by the Holy Spirit. If we do not surrender to the refiner's fire, we will have no other choice but to once again cheapen the definition of revival.

We must remember that God has not called our churches to be houses of preaching or programs, but houses of prayer. It's not hard to understand why the enemy has tried to convince us all that prayer is boring. When our churches moved to a seeker-sensitive "entertainment" model, prayer stopped being the top priority. If your objective is to entertain people, you need a really excellent worship team and an up-and-coming celebrity preacher to hold the attention of the people.

Prayer meetings are not entertaining, but God has not called us to be entertained. He created us for open communication with Him through prayer. Friend, we cannot see the return of revival unless we become willing to see the return of prayer. Corey Russell of UPPERROOM said this: "Prayer is not boring; you are!"

We must open our churches for people to have personal times of prayer, and we must reinstate the prayer meeting as the most important meeting we host. Nothing is more important than making sure that Heaven's top priority becomes our top priority. It's time for us to admit that the entertainment models are not working. It's time for us to realign ourselves with what God wants from His people.

> *Even those I will bring to My holy mountain and make them joyful in My house of prayer. Their burnt offerings and their sacrifices will be acceptable on My altar; for My house will be called a house of prayer for all the peoples* (Isaiah 56:7).

When we make God's house a house of prayer, He will respond by making it a house of revival. His response to our surrender and our travail is to release His glory, marking a generation for eternity. This is the greatest longing of the human heart. We long for God's nearness, His power, and His glory. We want to do more than hear about God; we want to know Him and experience Him.

The fires of revival will burn once more when the anguish of intercession captures the hearts of God's people.

Let's take a moment and pray:

> *Father, in the name of Jesus, I submit my life to the refining process of the Holy Spirit. I don't want to short-circuit the work of prayer and repentance in my life. I want my life to be a reflection of who You are, and I want to be a person of perpetual prayer. Make me that person, in Jesus' name, amen.*

Chapter 4

THE MANIFESTATION OF GOD'S REPUTATION

Then the Lord spoke to Moses, saying, "Speak to Aaron and to his sons, saying, 'Thus you shall bless the sons of Israel. You shall say to them: The Lord bless you, and keep you; the Lord make His face shine on you, and be gracious to you; the Lord lift up His countenance on you, and give you peace.' So they shall invoke My name on the sons of Israel, and I then will bless them" (Numbers 6:22-27).

WHEN GOD MOVES BY His Spirit, He always does it with purpose. Revival never happens so that the saints can just enjoy some awesome services. God shows up to mark people with His very own identity. Far more is at stake in a move of God than whether or not you're going to have good church meetings, a great evangelist, wonderful apostolic leaders, and great worship leaders. In authentic revival, God takes a hot firebrand and burns it on to the spirits of those who come together, forever marking them with His name.

We must press in beyond the mentality that special services are going to win this world. We need something more than a better marketing strategy or another church-growth idea. We need the red-hot branding iron of the Holy Spirit to mark us so deeply that we care about His glory more than we care about our own ministries.

There has been so much self-promotion in the Church that I believe it has become a stench in the nostrils of God. Ministers have strutted like peacocks across platforms around the world, but especially in America. We tried to sanctify the American dream and call it Christian success, but the fancier our ministers have become, the more they have promoted themselves; the larger their social media footprints have become, the more we have seen the Holy Spirit grieved by man worship.

One of the great things about a move of God is that it brings us back to the concept that none of this is really about us, but it really all is for Jesus Christ. Ministers and preachers and hotshot worship leaders take a back seat to the mighty Holy Spirit, who comes to magnify the wonderful name of Jesus. One of the first things we notice in a move of God is that all of the focus is on the King and nothing else matters. It has always been this way throughout Scripture and in church history. God desires to place His name on a people who have been sanctified unto Him.

Allow me to say it like this: God wants to put His name, His reputation, back on His Church. Oh, we have had enough of ourselves! The headlines have been filled with ministers who have fallen because they forgot that Jesus Christ will come to have first place in all things. We need to stop worrying about our "brand" and let the branding of God come upon us. He wants to put His name on us!

In Numbers 6, God instructs Moses and Aaron on how to bless the people. This is a precious passage of Scripture because it shows us that the key to God's blessing was and is His reputation. Aaron was instructed to describe God's reputation, His graciousness, His compassion, His peace, and so on. In describing God's nature over the people, God said, "So they will put My name on My people, and I will bless them." By blessing those who were in covenant with Yahweh, the priests were putting God's name, His reputation, on the people. By receiving the blessing of the priests, God's people were receiving His name.

As His covenant people, the people of Israel were witnesses to what God could do. They had enjoyed a front-row seat to see some of His most spectacular wonders. They were living proof that if you were in covenant with God and you needed Him to set you free, He was more than willing to blow up a superpower (Egypt) to fulfill His promise of freedom to them.

He even used the wilderness to demonstrate His nature to Israel and through them. They became the living proof that God's name, His reputation, is Jehovah Jireh, the God who sees our needs and provides for them in advance. In a wilderness where they could not get their own food, God literally chose to rain down bread from Heaven to meet their need. He was showing everyone around them that He is a good Father. Why does this matter? Because in John chapter 6, Jesus said, "I am the bread that came down from Heaven." This was not just a call to dinner; it was a demonstration of God's reputation!

In a land that was known for being dry and for going without rain for extended amounts of time, the book of 1 Corinthians tells us that a rock followed Israel through the wilderness, gushing gallons of water each and every day so that the people of Israel would not die of thirst in that wilderness. Paul makes no bones about it. He says, "and the rock was Christ Jesus!" This was not just a meeting of a need, but it was a demonstration that Jesus Christ Himself is the living water that quenches the thirst of every weary soul who will simply take a drink.

Even though they did not have it all together, even though they grumbled and complained, God still chose to put His reputation on those people. He became known to the nations as the God of Israel. Because of how He delivered them from Egyptian bondage, raining down plagues upon the wicked pharaoh who opposed them, the nations recognized Yahweh as the God who held power.

Many times in my own life, I have found myself frustrated with how God works. I wish I could claim that I really have a handle on the whole "patience" thing, but more often than not, I want to hurry God along. I want things to happen on my timetable. Waiting for God's timing is just not a lot of fun. I have to think Israel would have struggled with that too.

You see, when God finally came down to deliver Israel out of Egypt, they had been in bondage for just over four hundred years. That is staggering! Generations of Israelites had lived and died in chains, coming under the whips of their wicked Egyptian taskmasters. Mothers had given birth to children in chains. There was no freedom to make decisions. There was no empathy from the Egyptians. There was only cruel toil under a hot, desert sun.

How frustrated do you think they were with God? What could God be thinking? Why was He letting their slavery continue?

I think Israel had done what a lot of us do: they had forgotten the part of the prophetic word that they did not like. We have selective hearing. We remember what we want to remember, but when life starts getting real, we feel like God has let us down. Israel remembered Genesis 12:3: "*And I will bless those who bless you, and the one who curses you I will curse. And in you all the families of the earth will be blessed.*" They had forgotten this part in Genesis 15:13-14:

> *God said to Abram, "Know for certain that your descendants will be strangers in a land that is not theirs, where they will be enslaved and oppressed four hundred years. But I will also judge the nation whom they will serve, and afterward they will come out with many possessions."*

The slavery was just as much a part of the prophetic destiny of Israel as the blessing was. God had allowed their slavery to hit the boiling point of four hundred years. He had allowed their slavery to accumulate because, by the time God stepped in, nobody but the Almighty God Himself could have gotten Israel out of bondage. They had no resources, no battle skills, no allies, and no hope. God used their nightmare to not only set them free, but to show His reputation to the nations all around them. Suddenly, entire nations knew that Yahweh was not a God who sat on a shelf, but a throne. They knew that this was the God who does wonders. To this day, every time you sing, "Waymaker, miracle worker, promise keeper, light in the darkness," you are referencing the fact that God made a way for His people where there seemed to be no way.

And this is the God who wants to put His name on your life. The same One who parted the sea wants to sanctify you unto Himself, calling you His child.

I want us to recognize that Aaron would bless the people, thus putting God's name on them. Then, God would bless the people for the sake of His own name. It's time for us to remember that everything God has ever done, everything He is doing on the earth right now, and everything He ever will do, is all done in the interest of His own great name.

God does not send revival to increase our own reputation. It's not about our increase or our need for attention. God sends revival to clearly magnify the wonderful name of Jesus Christ. Perhaps the reason He has waited so long to send another great awakening to the nations is similar to what Israel went through. No one but God will get the credit for this! God is about to mark you with His reputation. He wants to put His name on you!

The easiest way I know of to get a new name is to simply be born. When you come into this world, you receive your name before you even have the ability to understand anything.

My husband, Nathan, is originally from the United Kingdom. He's a good Yorkshire Brit, and somehow God made the man marry a Georgia peach. It has been nothing if not an adventure! When He came to the USA and we got married, he applied for a green card, which gave him permanent resident status in America. I wish you could see the amount of paperwork that we had to complete just for that application. I filled out more paperwork to marry that man than I have ever done to apply for a mortgage. We had to pay fees. We had to have his retinas and fingerprints scanned. We had to be interviewed to make sure that I was not just smuggling Englishmen into the country. I remember feeling so much relief when the interviewer granted us a two-year green card. We had worked hard for it!

Two years later, we had to pay another fee, get more scans, and we had to be interviewed again. They asked me, "Do you still like him?"

I said, "Yes, I do, and if it's all the same to y'all, I'd like to keep him." They granted us another green card.

Then he applied for United States citizenship. We paid another fee. We got more scans. He had another interview, but this time he was tested on his knowledge of USA civics. I will never forget the day that he was able to pledge allegiance to my nation and was granted all the rights and privileges that I enjoy. That moment meant so much to Nathan and me because we had paid a price and been tested.

But when our little boys were born, from the first breath of oxygen that filled their lungs, they were immediately United States citizens. Because they were associated with my name, they received effortlessly what their father had had to work for and be tested on. They didn't pay a price; they just received the name!

I said God wants to put His name on you!

Another great way to receive a new name is to be adopted. When my brother and his wife adopted their little boy, the problems of the family name that he had been born with were officially no more. Instead of the strife and trauma of his birth family, that little boy received the name of a family that has generations in ministry. He did not work for it or pay for it, but his parents put on his life a family name that has a history in God.

Are you beginning to understand? You see, Paul says that we have been brought into the family of God through the Spirit of adoption. My goodness—that would be enough! But Jesus Himself said, "You must be born again." That means that God wants us to have both the name and the spiritual DNA to back it up. He wants us to walk in His reputation!

The other way to receive a new name is through marriage. When I walked down the aisle to marry Nathan, suddenly a girl from Georgia who speaks with a strong Southern accent was immediately associated with a Yorkshire family from the UK, a family that has generations of history. They're prim and proper and delightfully British, but through the covenant of marriage, they are stuck with a daughter-in-law who is as American as apple pie.

You may not feel worthy and you may not feel ready, but I came to tell you that God is about to manifest His reputation on His sons and daughters who have been born again, adopted, and who are now a part of His bride. You are going to get a new name!

As we look deeper into this concept, we see that all throughout Scripture, God would point to the coming of the Messiah by describing His reputation. I'm reminded of the prophet Isaiah, who arguably had the clearest prophetic glimpse of Jesus before His incarnation. God wanted Israel to recognize their Messiah and to receive Him, so He revealed Himself to Isaiah by His reputation. Isaiah stood up and proclaimed, "*For a child will be born to us, a son will be given to us, and the government will rest on His shoulders, and His name will be called Wonderful Counselor, Mighty God, Eternal Father, the Prince of Peace*" (Isaiah 9:6).

It's as though God was shouting to the people of Israel, "You will know My Son by My reputation!" He proclaimed God's desire to dwell among His people by saying, "You will call His name Emmanuel," which means "God with us." God was going to allow His Son to be born of a virgin and walk among us, live among us, and teach among us, all to demonstrate the reputation of Yahweh in an up-close and personal kind of way.

To take this a step even further, let's talk about how the Hebrew culture named their children. When a child was born, the parents did not just choose a name that sounded nice; they chose the name of the child by the meaning. The meaning of the name would point to the destiny of the child. This is demonstrated all throughout the Word of God.

Abraham and Sarah named their son "Isaac," which means "laughter." God had brought them the joy of having their son, even though Sarah had laughed at the impossibility of God's Word coming to pass. God gave the prophet Isaiah specific names for his children, and those names provided prophetic pictures to Israel.

One of my favorite pictures of this is found in the birth of John the Baptist. His father and mother were Zachariah and Elizabeth. How did we know that their offspring would be the forerunner of the Christ? Zachariah's name means, "Yahweh remembers," and Elizabeth's name means, "the oath God swore." When God remembered the oath He swore to Abraham that through Abraham's seed the nations would be blessed, the forerunner was born to announce the coming of the One who would fulfill that promise.

This is why Mary and Joseph were not allowed to name the Lord Jesus. Think about this: God trusted Mary and Joseph implicitly. He trusted them to raise His Son in their house, with their family. He trusted them to steward this precious gift to the world. He did not even give them parenting advice! They may have needed some counsel, because they literally lost the Son of God for three days! I have had some bad parenting days, but I have never lost my kids for three days. Can you imagine it?!

But while God trusted Mary and Joseph to raise His Son, He did not trust them to name Him, because they would have given Him a name that would have prophesied their own desires. At that moment of history, Israel was expecting the Messiah to show up and defeat the Romans, giving Israel back their land and their autonomy. They had a great understanding of the Messiah ruling the world at His second coming, but they did not understand the first coming at all. They were wanting Messiah to do something political, but He came to do something eternal.

If God the Father had allowed Mary and Joseph to name the baby, they would have prophesied according to their own perception and expectation of what the Messiah should do.

But it's as though God were saying, "No, you can't tamper with My reputation. You can't prophesy according to what you want. Since I am the Father, I will be the one to prophesy My Son's nature. You will call His name Jesus!"

When God sent Gabriel to announce Jesus to Mary, God took that opportunity to announce the name of Jesus, but also to describe His reputation.

> *The angel said to her, "Do not be afraid, Mary; for you have found favor with God. And behold, you will conceive in your womb and bear a son, and you shall name Him Jesus. He will be great and will be called the Son of the Most High; and the Lord God will give Him the throne of His father David; and He will reign over the house of Jacob forever, and His kingdom will have no end"* (Luke 1:30-33).

Of all the names that God the Father could have chosen to put on His Son, to declare the prophetic destiny of this One who would be salvation to the nations, He chose the name "Yeshua."

The Hebrew meaning of *Yeshua* is "salvation, deliverance, help, victory, prosperity." "The primary meaning is "to rescue from distress or danger." God wanted us to easily recognize His Son, so He named Him salvation!

It's not just that Jesus saves; He saves because His name is salvation! Deliverance is not just an action He performs; it is His identity! He does not just help us; He Himself is the Help! It's like that song says, "Victory has a name, and it's Jesus!" His identity is my salvation. His reputation is the power that sets me free.

When you begin to understand this truth, it starts changing how you pray for revival. For instance, I don't have to talk God into demonstrating His healing power so that a meeting will be better. I don't have to hope that Jesus is in the mood to heal today. One of His names, one of the earmarks of His reputation, is that He is Jehovah Rapha, the Lord our Healer! When He shows up, He leaves evidence of His presence. One of the greatest hindrances we have seen against believers is the enemy afflicting them with sickness and disease. God's people have dealt with so much infirmity. I believe it's time for the Church to rise up in the power of the name, the reputation of Jesus Christ, and say, "The Lord is our Healer right now! We are not subject to sickness any longer."

When I pray for revival, I frequently use breakthrough language. I'm sure you will agree that the USA and so many nations are in desperate need of a supernatural breakthrough, but I don't have to talk God into sending breakthrough, because He Himself is the breakthrough! In 2 Samuel 5:20, one of God's names was revealed as, "The Lord of the Breakthrough."

You see it's not that we need salvation; we need Jesus the Savior. We don't just need healing; we need Jesus the Healer. We don't just need deliverance; we need Jesus the Deliverer! We don't just need breakthrough; we need Jesus Himself who, according to Micah 2:13, is the Breaker who goes up before us. We don't just need revival, where the dead church comes back to life, we need Jesus who declared in John 14:6 that He is the resurrection and the life!

Friend, the more we understand His wonderful name, His glorious reputation, the more we find ourselves reducing our prayer life to Jesus. Oh, how we need Him! And how astounded we should be to marvel at this truth: He wants to put *that name* on us!

Psalm 149:4 says, "*For the Lord takes pleasure in His people; He will beautify the afflicted ones with salvation.*"

That word *salvation* is actually the Hebrew word for salvation—*yeshua*. He wants to beautify our little messed up lives with His own reputation.

His name points directly to His character! When I call on the name of Jesus, I am associating myself with what He has made known about His nature. When we pray in the name of Jesus, we are not just using His name as a tagline to end our prayer. It's not some magic wand. Praying in the name of Jesus enforces God's reputation on our circumstances! If you are sick, rebuking your sickness in Jesus' name causes that sickness to bow to Christ's reputation as the Healer. If you need a financial miracle, praying in His name causes your lack to bow to His reputation as a good Father and Provider.

When I call upon the name of Jesus, I am causing His reputation to be superimposed on my situation. That is why Jeremiah 33:3 says, "*Call to Me and I will answer you, and I will tell you great and mighty things, which you do not know.*" When we call on the name of Jesus, revelation is the normal response.

Being a person of prayer does not mean that we deny our circumstances, but it does mean that we deny our circumstances the power to dictate our level of joy! We don't function on the emotional roller coaster of this world, because we trust in the name of the Lord our God!

Jesus' high priestly prayer for His disciples and for all of us who would come to know Him included a plea to the Father for us to stay in His reputation.

> *I am no longer in the world; and yet they themselves are in the world, and I come to You. Holy Father, keep them in Your name, the name which You have given Me, that they may be one even as We are* (John 17:11).

Our confidence in prayer is that when we ask according to Jesus' reputation, the Father will grant our request so that His Son might be glorified. Jesus Himself said this in John 15:16:

> *You did not choose Me but I chose you, and appointed you that you would go and bear fruit, and that your fruit would remain, so that whatever you ask of the Father in My name He may give to you.*

As our world plunges into deeper darkness and the second coming of the Lord Jesus draws closer, we must understand the importance of His reputation. When we stay within the confines of His name, living our lives in the light of His reputation, we find His name to be our place of safety. The Bible says in Proverbs 18:10, "*The name of the Lord is a strong tower; the righteous runs into it and is safe.*" His name is our refuge!

There is no name more powerful than the name of Jesus Christ! There is power in the name of Jesus. At His great name, every power of darkness must bow. At His name, miracles happen and hope is restored. At His name, oppression must go and healing must come. There has never been, nor will there ever be a name like the matchless name of Jesus Christ! When we cry out for revival, we are asking for His name to be revealed once again, branded onto our hearts for eternity, with all the evidence of His nature being manifested in our lives.

This world does not need another presentation. What it needs is a fresh demonstration of the name of Jesus, because Paul tells us that the name of Jesus is the highest name, the name that every knee will bow before and every tongue confess. Philippians 2:5-11 says:

> *Have this attitude in yourselves which was also in Christ Jesus, who, although He existed in the form of God, did not regard equality with God a thing to be grasped, but emptied Himself, taking the form of a bond-servant, and being made in the likeness of men. Being found in appearance as a man, He humbled Himself by becoming obedient to the point of death, even death on a cross. For this reason also, God highly exalted Him, and bestowed on Him the name which is above every name, so that at the name of Jesus every knee will bow, of those who are in heaven and on earth and under the earth, and that every tongue will confess that Jesus Christ is Lord, to the glory of God the Father.*

We could rightly say that a major aspect of revival is when we begin to see the manifestation of God's reputation working among us again. My friend, this wonderful Jesus wants to put His name on you. Wherever you are right now, wherever you're reading this, I invite you to bow your whole life to Him.

Tell Him:

> *Lord Jesus, I want my heart to burn for You. I want*

my life to be marked for eternity. I want You to put Your reputation on my life, so that whatever comes of my life, only You will receive the glory. Amen.

Chapter 5

THE CONVERGENCE: WHEN HEAVEN AND EARTH COLLIDE

REVIVAL PRAYING IS WHEN we begin to cry out and travail for nothing less than Heaven touching earth. We want to see the reality of God on the Throne permeating every area of our life until it touches our government, our schools, our homes, and our children.

Friend, this is something worth praying about. This takes prayer out of the realm of seeing how much stuff we can convince God to give us, and takes it into the place of holy desperation, where we don't stop contending until we see everything around us shift.

Several years ago, the Lord spoke a word to me that I must confess I did not fully understand. Sometimes, the Lord speaks to me, and then I get out my dictionary app. I heard the Holy Spirit thunder on the inside of me, "There is a convergence!" I knew that God was saying something that was both crucial and specific, so I hurried to get out that app. Here is what I found when I looked up the word *converge*. Converge: to tend or move toward one point or one another, come together, meet, to come together and unite in a common interest or focus.

Then I understood what the Holy Spirit was saying to me. This is what we are praying for! We are standing in faith for the great coming together, for when God pours out His Spirit, for the moment when Heaven touches earth and we are irrevocably changed!

I am looking for the head-on collision of Heaven and earth, where everything around us looks like the second chapter of Acts and Jesus is the only name that gets the credit for it. Revival is when the supernatural Holy Spirit invades our natural lives and uses us to magnify Jesus Christ. It's when suddenly we see the fulfillment of things God promised us years ago.

In the South, when we prepare the evening meal we say, "We're fixing dinner." Some of my friends from the North would probably laugh at that phraseology and ask, "Why, is it broken?" But any good Southerner would say, "Hush and go get ready for dinner." We don't worry about what people think of our terminology, because we can probably cook better than they can anyway.

One of my favorite passages of Scripture is in the book of Genesis, chapter 18, when God showed up at Abraham's house, and Abraham said to the Lord, "If now I have found favor in Your sight, please do not pass your servant by." I want you to see that this is a revival prayer, an invitation for a head-on collision with the presence and purpose of God. Abraham would not let God move past him. He insisted on fellowship with God as a necessity.

I can hardly wrap my mind around what happened next. Abraham and Sarah started fixing dinner for God Himself! Can you imagine it? I mean, it's wild enough that God showed up on the doorstep, but how in the world did they decide what to cook for Him? How did Sarah set the table? What do you put on the plate when God comes for dinner?

The Word of God indicates that Abraham took the position of a waiter, serving the Lord and the two angels that had come with Him. You see, when God comes to fellowship with you, if you serve Him in humility, you will provoke a conversation that will forever change the trajectory of your life, as Abraham and Sarah soon found out. Abraham's posture of humility caused God to push back from the table and begin to ask some serious questions.

> *Then they said to him, "Where is Sarah your wife?" And he said, "There, in the tent." He said, "I will surely return to you at this time next year; and behold, Sarah your wife will have a son." And Sarah was listening at the tent door, which was behind him. Now Abraham and Sarah were old, advanced in age; Sarah was past childbearing. Sarah laughed to herself, saying, "After I have become old, shall I have pleasure, my lord being old also?" And the Lord said to Abraham, "Why did Sarah laugh, saying, 'Shall I indeed bear a child, when I am so old?' Is anything too difficult for the Lord? At the appointed time I will return to you, at this time next year, and Sarah will have a son"* (Genesis 18:9-14).

You see, friend, the original promise of God to Abraham—that he would have descendants as numerous as the stars in the heavens—had occurred about twenty-four years before this dinner conversation. In that time, Abraham and Sarah had so many opportunities to become discouraged. God had made them a promise, but God had not told them how long they were going to have to wait for the fulfillment. Even at the dinner table, God told them, "You will hold this baby one year from now."

Before you decide to work Sarah over for laughing at this word from the Lord, let's take a moment to place ourselves in her shoes. She is 89 years old, and there is no physically possible way for this word to come true for her. It sounds ridiculous, and yes, it is laughable. It was impossible when the Lord had spoken it twenty-four years ago, but now it's almost painful to even think about it.

But no matter how impossible it sounds, no matter how out of reach the fulfillment of God's word for your life seems, I'm here to tell you that there is a moment coming when the fulfillment of God's decree over your life catches up to where you are. There is a convergence!

God has spoken some things over your life, and it's time to let those things catch up to the moment you're living in. I came to tell you that God has said things about you, your family, your church, this city, and this nation. You have languished long enough. You have waited long enough! It is time to appropriate what God has decreed! It's time to get your hands on the fulfillment of the promise of God over your life. God is not a man that He should lie or change His mind. He will do what He has promised. It's time for you to believe again!

Discouragement and delay like to join hands and come against God's people together. When we have to wait for God's promise to be fulfilled, we become frustrated. All my life, I have heard people speak about a mighty end-time move of God that will flood the nations of this world with the knowledge of the glory of God. While I have seen glimpses, I have not yet seen the total fulfillment of that word. I want to! Oh, it would be easy to become discouraged and frustrated. But we must not lose heart. In Galatians 6:9, Paul said, "*Let us not lose heart in doing good, for in due time we will reap if we do not grow weary.*"

See, God had taken Abraham on a journey. Many times, if God speaks a word or gives a promise for our lives, He will require you to begin a journey that will initially reduce you.

Abraham started his journey by taking his nephew, Lot, along with him. God had specifically told Abraham to go away from his family and his people, but Abraham decided to take Lot along. That presented all kinds of problems. Lot was not interested in paying the price to know God for himself; he simply wanted to hang around the blessing. God had to remove Lot and the baggage he came with from his life so that Abraham could be ready to receive the promise.

Why do we see a delay on the promise of revival? I believe that often it's because we are dragging a lot of heavy baggage around with us and trying to pretend we have it all together. We don't want anyone to notice that we are still carrying around hurt and drama from our family. We don't want people to know that we're fighting the temptation to "help" God out with the fulfillment of His Word. When you have to wait a long time to receive what God said, your greatest temptations will be to hide your baggage and to try to help God.

When Abraham and Sarah tried to help God out, Sarah gave Abraham her maid, Hagar. Abraham went along with this plan without uttering so much as one word of prayer about it. This was not a faith decision. This was a choice made entirely on the premise, "I'm afraid God won't be able to do what He has promised, so I have prepared this lovely backup plan." Their backup plan gave birth to Ishmael, and it caused all hell to break out in their family. Their fear-based decision gave birth to strife and bitterness, because that is what fear always produces. Fear will always reproduce according to its nature. Fear-based decisions will never give birth to faith-based results.

To tell the truth, if you have an Ishmael in your life, that is proof positive that you have given up on your Isaac. Think about this: when God showed up to Abraham's tent for dinner that day, Ishmael was old enough that he was probably playing out in the yard. Abraham did not try to hide what his fear had produced. He had to live with it every day. And even though Ishmael was walking evidence that Abraham had given up, God still came to dinner at his tent, sat down at the table, and provoked his faith back to life.

I want you to know, friend, you may have an Ishmael in your life. You may have given up on the promise of God to your life, but I have wonderful news for you: God has not given up on you! When He speaks to your life, when He makes a promise, He is counting on His own great faithfulness to supply the fulfillment of His Word, not yours. He will always speak to you to provoke the revival of your faith, even when He sees the evidence of your doubt. Stop trying to hide your unbelief and ask the Lord to help it! Just like the father of the boy who was demonized, cry out, "Lord, I believe! Help my unbelief." He answers those prayers!

I want us to notice something else that occurred on Abraham's journey. When he first set out, he was called "Abram," which means "father." But when he came into covenant with Yahweh, he received a brand-new name. God changed his name to "Abraham," which means "father of nations." Most of us would have been content with the first name, right? Why was it so necessary for him to be called Abraham?

God wanted Abraham to know that this covenant was about a lot more than his own little family. This was not just about Abraham and Sarah holding a baby boy. God wanted to pull him up into a higher conversation, into the big picture. It's as though God was saying, "It's not enough for you to just be a father to your little family. You have to be one who births nations."

I believe that many of us have stopped short of authentic revival so many times, because we thought God was primarily concerned with us birthing something in our own churches or ministries. When will we realize that God wants to shift entire cities, regions, and nations with His glory? It's not just about our little circle; He wants to break yokes of bondage off of nations and people groups. He wants to sweep through counties and cities with the mighty flow of the Holy Spirit! We are going to have to start cooperating with Heaven's big-picture mentality.

God's perspective is so much different than ours! He doesn't see you as who you are right now. He sees the person He is developing you into! He sees your destiny! We serve the God who knows the end from the beginning. He finishes a thing before He begins it.

It's not enough for you to call yourself Abram. It's not enough for you to stop short on your destiny like your grandfather did. It's not enough for you to be who you've always been! It's time for your identity to align itself with the Word from Heaven! It's time for everything to recalibrate according to God's Word! God is going to take you from Abram to Abraham. He's going to take you out of where you've always been and put you where He has always intended you to be. Friend, by the time God places that answered prayer into your hands, you might not be who you have always been!

The process, the journey that God is taking you on is not to keep you from seeing the answer to your prayer. The purpose of the journey is to make you ready to receive what God has for you. Your convergence, your head-on collision with God's purpose for your life, has an appointment. There is an intersection between time and eternity, and it's got your name on it!

> *There is an appointed time for everything. And there is a time for every event under heaven* (Ecclesiastes 3:1).

There is a moment when the eternal Word catches up with time. There comes a collision between earth and Heaven. You might call it a divine interruption. You might call it a suddenly. Right now in the Western world, we are standing in an intersection waiting for a massive head-on collision between earth and Heaven. I believe we are going to call it *awakening!*

We must have a great awakening! We've got to have a culture-shifting, government-rocking, society-shaking move of God! There have been plenty of words from God that this is what's coming. Many have talked about it, prayed about it, fasted for it, and believed for it. But I believe it's time for the convergence! It's time for the collision.

If I were to be completely honest, the two revivals that I was allowed to see only shifted church culture a bit. They did not proceed to change the culture of the United States. I'm not blaming anyone or trying to cause a problem; I'm just telling the truth. Years later, can we tell that those moves of God happened? I thank God for every life that was touched, but I am not asking Him to let me see more localized revival meetings. I want to see something happen that changes the culture so much, it won't matter what church you walk into. I want to see the government begin to pass righteous legislation that lines up with the Word of God, because the hearts of the people have changed so much. I want to see music and entertainment change because they can no longer get away with the garbage they have propagated.

It's time for the convergence!

Maybe you're reading this and saying, "Lydia, I am in the waiting, and I don't want to become discouraged. What should I do?" While you're waiting for your fulfillment, your posture should be worship.

When God approached Abraham at the tent, the Bible says that Abraham "bowed himself" low to the ground. This is one of the Hebrew words for *worship*. Interestingly enough, this particular word has nothing to do with music. It is all about acknowledging God's superiority and His lordship over our lives. This is about humbling ourselves. It is the picture of Abraham bowing down in the dirt and looking up at God to say, "I bow my whole life to You. You are my King. I am in covenant with You, and I do not want You to pass me by."

It's hard to worship when you're in a waiting period. It's hard to give God your very best when it's costing you the very most. Anyone who tries to tell you that this is easy is straight up lying to you. This can be the most difficult posture to assume; however, when you worship from that place of desperate brokenness, it attracts the presence of God in a powerful way.

You see, when you wait upon the Lord, Isaiah 40:31 tells us that you receive new strength. But in verse 30, we learn that the Lord never gets tired. He never experiences fatigue. Even when others become exhausted, He never becomes weary. So when you worship, when you wait on the Lord, you receive renewed strength because you have stepped into His divine nature. In your own strength, you can become exhausted; but when you determine to worship in your waiting, you receive divine strength that carries you through to your convergence. Hallelujah!

Praise sets the table, but worship is the main course. It brings you to the table and it brings God to the table. God wants us to be people who know how to linger, to abide in His presence. Your waiting does not have to be wasted time. Use it to fellowship with the One who made the promise.

Abraham's worship made it possible for him to be an intercessor, and the intercessory conversation that he had with the Lord resulted in the direct rescue of Lot from Sodom. If Abraham had not interceded, Lot would have died; but if Abraham had not worshiped, he would not have been able to access intercession. Abraham shows us a crucial pattern here: before you intercede, you should worship. Before you come asking, you should come giving.

The culture of today's Western Church would turn on a dime if we would simply shift our thinking from trying to get God to please us to us trying to please God. We must remember that the King is on the Throne, and it is all about Him!

> *But an hour is coming, and now is, when the true worshipers will worship the Father in spirit and truth; for such people the Father seeks to be His worshipers. God is spirit, and those who worship Him must worship in spirit and truth* (John 4:23-24).

If you want to be the one God is looking for, you must worship! Your worship could be setting the table for a conversation that will affect the destiny of nations.

When worship is your priority, intercession is your privilege. Those who have been intimate with God are the ones He converses with about His plans. When you've ministered to Him in worship, He can trust your prayer life to shift your nation. Friend, anyone whom God has used greatly in revival will tell you that before they were "discovered" in the public place, they had to learn to cultivate intimacy with God in the secret place.

As we worship our way into intercession, what then should we pray? What does a convergence prayer look like? I believe that Jesus Himself gave us the prayer that causes Heaven to collide with earth.

> *Pray, then, in this way: "Our Father who is in heaven, hallowed be Your name. Your kingdom come. Your will be done, on earth as it is in heaven. Give us this day our daily bread. And forgive us our debts, as we also have forgiven our debtors. And do not lead us into temptation, but deliver us from evil. [For Yours is the kingdom and the power and the glory forever. Amen]"* (Matthew 6:9-13).

Friend, when you pray, "Your kingdom come, Your will be done, on earth as it is in Heaven," it's like you're standing in the middle of an interstate inviting the great semitruck of Heaven to run into your life. This is the prayer that causes the fulfillment of the word of the Lord to run into your life. This is the prayer that makes you ready to receive it. This is the prayer that breaks the power of delay. And friend, believe me when I tell you, this is a prayer that brings revival!

Take a moment and pray with me:

Father, in the name of Jesus, I ask You to bring about the fulfillment of every word You have spoken over my life, my family, my church, my city, and my nation. Bring revival, bring awakening, and let my life be a mighty witness to Your great faithfulness. In Jesus' name, amen.

Chapter 6

THE DRIVING FORCE OF HUNGER

Oh, that men would give thanks to the Lord for His goodness, and for His wonderful works to the children of men! For He satisfies the longing soul, and fills the hungry soul with goodness (Psalm 107:8-9 NKJV).

THIS IS ONE OF the most wonderful aspects of God's nature: He loves to satisfy the longing soul, filling it with His own goodness! He is the source of everything good and satisfying. So many times, we have seen the Church run on empty, simply because we have hungered for everything but the Lord. But if we are going to see revival, it is going to come to those who have cultivated a gut-level hunger for Jesus Himself.

I looked up the word *hunger* in the dictionary, and here's what I found: "a compelling need or desire for food. The painful sensation or state of weakness caused by the need for food; a shortage of food; famine. A strong or compelling desire or craving."

Hunger is one of the most crucial elements to the pursuit of revival and, ultimately, of God Himself. Jesus placed a premium on hunger when He spoke about it in the Sermon on the Mount. He said, "*Blessed are those who hunger and thirst for righteousness, for they shall be satisfied*" (Matthew 5:6).

It is hunger for God that drives us, compels us even, to cry out for revival until our lives are satiated with His presence. But hunger cannot be imparted. I cannot give you my hunger for God. I can't make you crave His presence. I wish I could.

It breaks my heart to hear so many believers use the language of hunger and desperation, but the evidence of their lives shows that it was only so much talk. We know how to sing songs about desperate hunger that only God can fill, yet we can only sing them for twenty minutes at church, or the congregation won't stay with us. We preach messages about longing for God, but we can't preach them for more than thirty minutes, or people will leave. That is not real hunger and thirst, so it will not be filled.

How many times have we said we were hungry for God, but in reality we were not willing to make more time for Him? Could it be that we say what we need to say at church to make ourselves look good? I do not want to reach the end of my life and realize that while I participated in a lot of church meetings, I never actually allowed myself to be satisfied by Jesus Christ.

My friend, there is such a thing as being satisfied in Christ! You don't have to be one more restless Christian, claiming His name and yet still trying to fill your life up with other things. You don't have to bounce from conference to conference hoping to get something new. The Ancient of Days wants to be your all in all.

Jesus knew the danger of people who knew how to talk the talk, but who were not really hungry for Him. When Jesus was ready to cull the crowd that followed Him, when He wanted to move past the casual followers to the committed disciples, He made this shocking announcement:

> *So Jesus said to them, "Truly, truly, I say to you, unless you eat the flesh of the Son of Man and drink His blood, you have no life in yourselves. He who eats My flesh and drinks My blood has eternal life, and I will raise him up on the last day. For My flesh is true food, and My blood is true drink. He who eats My flesh and drinks My blood abides in Me, and I in him. As the living Father sent Me, and I live because of the Father, so he who eats Me, he also will live because of Me. This is the bread which*

> *came down out of heaven; not as the fathers ate and died; he who eats this bread will live forever"* (John 6:53-58).

This is an extraordinary statement, because Jesus is demanding that our appetite experience a change. We have been compelled to consume the Lord! We've been invited to partake of the substance of Jesus, to take in who He is! Jesus clearly states that if you are not hungry for Him, for all that He is, you are not abiding in Him. You have no part of Him. What a strong statement for the Son of God to make! His disciples said in John 6:60, "*This is a difficult statement; who can listen to it?*" Commanding His followers to hunger for Him and to consume Him was a shocking message to preach, and they didn't feel like it was going over very well. John tells us in verse 66 that many of Jesus' disciples withdrew from Him because of this message. They stopped following Jesus because they could not imagine learning to feast on Him.

As it was then, so it is today. We have so many people who are willing to follow the Lord from a distance, but when He demands all, when He commands us to feast only at His table, people withdraw. When we echo those commands of Jesus, we are told that we are intolerant and exclusive. Yes, of course, we are. We make no bones about it. There is only one of whom we can partake and receive the satisfaction of our souls, and His name is Jesus the Christ! He demands our all so that He can be our all, filling us up with all that He is. This is the invitation that is interwoven throughout the Word of God.

> *You shall set the bread of the Presence on the table before Me at all times* (Exodus 25:30).

God commanded the bread of His presence to be set before Him in the Tabernacle continually, because the Old Testament was intended to be types and shadows that point to Jesus. This Table of Showbread indicates to us that the bread of His presence is continually available to us, because Jesus has made Himself available to us through His death, burial, and resurrection.

Jesus wants us to feast on Him at all times. We have been invited to sit at His table and continually be satisfied with all that He is. The Bread of Presence is a meal of intimacy, where the light of His face shines on us and we receive of His divine nature. John 1:14 tells us that He is the Word made flesh, so *to consume the Lord is to enjoy His presence and to feast on His Word.*

At the table of the Lord, we find acceptance. We could never have earned a seat at this glorious table; it was purchased with the precious blood of Jesus. It is His grace that has brought us in and invited us to partake of the love of the Father.

At the table of the Lord, we find peace. Whether that was your family's history or not, at this table, there is no strife, no drama, no exploitation. At this table, there is wholeness and deep unity.

At the table of His presence, we find joy unspeakable and full of glory. Oh, thank God, it goes beyond happiness! It is so deep that the enemy cannot touch it or diminish it. As the old song says, "This joy that I have...the world didn't give it and the world can't take it away!"

At the table of the Lord, we find revelation, because the table of His presence is illuminated by the light of Holy Spirit's revelation. The more we consume the Lord, the more His

Spirit will unveil the nature of Jesus to us, causing us to respond in adoration. This is a table worth coming to!

At the table of the Lord, we find brothers and sisters, people God has assigned us to love and to grow with. We cannot even begin to understand what true family is until we sit at the table of the Lord with the blood-washed children of God.

In the definition of hunger that we used at the beginning of this chapter, it stated that one aspect of hunger was a state of weakness. When you don't eat, you become weak. We can even take it farther than that: if you do not eat the right kinds of food, you will become malnourished, and that could result in other medical problems. Suffice it to say, we become unhealthy.

When we don't come to the table of the Lord to satisfy our hunger, we find ourselves in a weakened or powerless state.

We cannot continue to tolerate the powerless church! This is not a normal condition, and it certainly is not one that we have the right to excuse. In Acts 1:8, Jesus told the disciples to wait for the Holy Spirit, and He said: *"but you will receive power when the Holy Spirit has come upon you; and you shall be My witnesses both in Jerusalem, and in all Judea and Samaria, and even to the remotest part of the earth."* In other words, we cannot represent Jesus properly until He has filled us by His Spirit. We cannot rightly offer Jesus to those around us until we have been satisfied in Him.

John 1:16 says, *"For of His fullness we have all received, and grace upon grace."* How can we expect to represent Jesus Christ to this world until we have been satisfied in His presence? Spiritual weakness and collapse always come when we have filled ourselves with lesser things. We must receive of His fullness, of His layers of grace.

You will always move toward what you are hungry for. The truth be told, if you show me your bank statement and your cell phone, I can tell you what you are really hungry for. If you are really hungry for God, it will be quantifiable in your daily life. We need a return to authentic hunger in the Body of Christ! We need a hunger that surpasses words and pushes us toward the Lord.

We have learned all the Christian catchphrases, and we even know when to turn to our neighbor and say them. But no matter what we have said, we see the truth about our hunger by what we have been using to fill up our lives. For instance, I keep saying that I need to lose some weight. I have gained and lost weight before, so I know what to do. I know what it takes. I know how to eat right and I know how to exercise. But the truth is, I like pizza. I know that I need a salad, but I want a pizza. Until I learn the difference between a temporary craving and actual need-based hunger, it will not matter how many weight loss apps I download. I will continue to have a problem. Do you understand?

We say that we want God to move in our churches, but we are so addicted to the clock on the wall that we do not have time to wait on the Lord. We say that we want to move into deeper places in worship, but we are still worrying about what other people think of us. We say that we are hungry for Jesus, but when was the last time we feasted on His Word?

Most of our churches are moving toward filling chairs with people instead of filling people with Jesus. We will do anything to be trendy, while people are hungry for a genuine encounter with the God that we have told them is supernatural.

If you can explain everything that happens in your meetings, it is time to fast and pray until the unexplainable starts to happen. We need some services that we can only explain by saying, "Not by might, nor by power, but by My Spirit!" Where are the services where we leave saying, "Only God could have done that!" We need something to happen that cannot be replicated by man, but can only be produced by the mighty Holy Spirit! When was the last time God did something totally unexplainable in your church, and you were left breathlessly saying, "Wow!" We sing at the top of our lungs that God's grace is amazing, yet we are bored to tears with church meetings that show no evidence of hungry believers. There is no awe because there has been no hunger.

Satisfying spiritual hunger with the wrong nourishment causes our cravings to be bent. We move from hunger to a desire for instant gratification. God does not do McDonald's; He likes for things to marinate.

Your life would totally change if you stopped worrying so much about time. We want something to happen to us so fast so we can keep on moving with our life. But the best food I have ever eaten took hours to marinate. There certainly was not a drive-thru window at that restaurant.

We need God to reset our appetite so that we will hunger for only Him.

Hunger for God will always cause you to press forward despite the opinions of those around you. Simply put, hunger and dignity cannot coexist. When you really want God more than anything else, no matter how you are criticized for it, you will allow your hunger to drive you to the table of the Lord! You won't make lame excuses like, "We've never done it that way before." You won't allow yourself to worry if you have gone too far with your worship.

I had to learn a long time ago that I cannot worry about my dignity. My passion for God has offended religious people many times before, but this is what I know: my soul finds its satisfaction only in the presence of Jesus! Someone else's opinion about my passion is not my problem. I am determined that I am going to show up to the Table of the Lord, where He has prepared a place for me to feast on Him.

I have learned that people who are hungry for God do not have time to be offended. The urgent need for God outweighs everything else.

When I am truly hungry for God, I don't allow your issues to become offensive to me. I don't get mad because someone didn't design a service for my comfort. When I'm hungry for Jesus, I understand that all this is for His glory, not mine.

We must return to designing a service to minister to the Lord, and when His presence comes, we feast at His table. Offense and passion for God cannot dwell together, because the person who is hungry for God forgives quickly so they can return to the table of the Lord.

Churches whose predominant culture is hunger for God tend to be kingdom-minded. They don't care if God is being poured out at their church or yours, as long as Jesus is there and His name is being lifted high.

I can't tell you how many times I have seen people stay out of revival services for no better reason than that they felt if God was really involved, He would have been using them. What arrogance! When you really love God, His presence, His Spirit, you don't care which of His children is being used to fill up your plate. You just get in line!

When you are really hungry, you do something about it. Real hunger for God will always produce an action. It will cause you to go after Him when no one else sees the necessity.

In the years following the Brownsville Revival, when people have heard me share my testimony, I have had so many people who lived in relatively close proximity to Pensacola tell me, "I wish I could have gotten there."

My heart sinks every time I hear that. I have been told that by people who lived much closer than my family did. It's heartbreaking! I always want to ask, "What was it that you thought was more important than encountering Jesus in a major outpouring?" The harsh, but simple truth is this: the hungry ones are the ones who showed up.

Hunger for God is not an emotion. It is a driving force that causes us to pursue God more than anything else. When you're not hungry for God, it is usually because you have been filling yourself with lesser things.

Spiritual appetite suppressants are so numerous right now. They can be really good things that you would never even suspect, but anything that divides your focus from Jesus to something else is the enemy of your spiritual appetite! You must take an aggressive stance against anything that competes with Jesus for your attention.

Hunger will move you beyond insecurity, because your hunger will bring you to the table of the Lord. We have a guarantee from God's Word that every hungry soul will find a place set for them at His table, and all are welcome to eat until they are satisfied. Hunger for God is the great equalizer. We all sit at the same table partaking of the same wonderful Jesus. None of us is better than anyone else.

You see, hunger for God produces humility. It says, "I humble myself. I acknowledge my weakness. Only You can sustain my life." It is only when we humble ourselves that we find real intimacy with God.

Hunger will drive you to a place of prayer while everyone else is seeking a platform. Prayer that changes nations occurs first in the secret place when no one else is watching. It has nothing to do with auditioning for a ministry position.

I love when I feel the tug of the Holy Spirit drawing me to pray. I love when He meets me in that place. I promise you this: I love being with Jesus more than I love preaching or leading worship or going to the nations. If I can't have Him, the rest of this is useless. We cannot afford to silence the whispers of the Holy Spirit! Let Him draw you close to Jesus. Only then will your soul be truly and deeply satisfied.

Pray this with me:

> *Father, in the name of Your Son, Jesus, I ask You to revive my hunger for You and Your righteousness. Oh, God, make me hungry again! I want to feast on the beauty of Christ Jesus until my soul is satisfied at the table of the Lord. Let my hunger drive me closer to You, in Jesus' name, amen.*

Chapter 7

HOSTING THE HOLY

Now David again gathered all the chosen men of Israel, thirty thousand. And David arose and went with all the people who were with him to Baale-judah, to bring up from there the ark of God which is called by the Name, the very name of the Lord of hosts who is enthroned above the cherubim. They placed the ark of God on a new cart that they might bring it from the house of Abinadab which was on the hill; and Uzzah and Ahio, the sons of Abinadab, were leading the new cart. So they brought it with the ark of God from the house of Abinadab, which was on the hill; and Ahio was walking ahead of the ark. Meanwhile, David and all the house of Israel were celebrating before the Lord with all kinds of instruments made of fir wood, and with lyres, harps, tambourines, castanets and cymbals.

But when they came to the threshing floor of Nacon, Uzzah reached out toward the ark of God and took hold of it, for the oxen nearly upset it. And the anger of the Lord burned against Uzzah, and God struck him down there for his irreverence; and he died there by the ark of God. David became angry because of the Lord's outburst against Uzzah, and that place is called Perez-uzzah to this day (2 Samuel 6:1-8).

FROM THE TIME I was a little girl, I have always loved to learn about David. His life provokes me to know God more. I read his victories and his failures, I read his love songs to the Lord, and I am blown away at the consistency of his passion over his lifetime. He did not do everything right, but he was known as a man after God's own heart. Not only that, but it was God Himself who described David that way. Friend, I don't know about you, but I want God to think of my heart for Him that same way. What a powerful commendation from Heaven!

David was called a man after God's own heart because he loved to minister to the Lord, and he placed a high priority on hosting God's presence. This is a golden key for those of us who are hungry for revival. Revival brings the nearness of God so close in our everyday life, so we must develop the same kind of passion that David had. We must determine in our hearts that we are going to host God in our own life, in our homes, and in our churches.

If there is one thing, one lesson that I have learned from experiencing and studying revival, it is this: God comes and stays where He is hosted well. God is not interested in being an entertaining addition to our Sunday services. He is interested in creating a habitation among those who give Him the preeminence that He so richly deserves.

Many churches fall so sadly short of experiencing the manifested presence of God because they are not trying to host Him; they're trying to host people. David cared about the people of Israel, but Scripture shows us that God's heart was his top priority.

When David came to the throne after the death of Saul, that marked a tectonic shift in policy and priority for the kingdom. David's ascension to the throne united the kingdoms of Israel and Judah, bringing unity where there had been civil war. There were many major differences in the leadership styles of David and Saul, but I believe the most important difference was found in this heart issue of pursuing God's presence.

David and the people of Israel were hungry for the presence of God. They had gone quite a while without sensing the need for His presence, because Saul was a man who thought he could rule without being in God's presence.

When we look closely at the life of Saul, we see such wasted God-given talent. We see that he was appointed, he was anointed, but he chose the path of arrogance. He started well. He was God's first choice for the rulership of Israel. Israel asked for a king, but it was God who selected Saul. When he became king, we read of the Spirit of the Lord coming upon him, and he would defeat the Philistines. We read of a king who was little in his own eyes, but the longer he stayed in power, the more he thought he had put himself there. Most alarmingly, we have no record in the Word of God of King Saul having a passion for God's presence. He was not a man of worship or prayer. He was not a student of God's Word. He really thought he could rule God's people outside of fellowship with Yahweh.

When we come to a place where we think we can continue with our lives outside of fellowship with the Lord, we are in the most severe kind of spiritual danger known to man. If you are satisfied with your own qualifications and giftings, that is all you will have to rely on, and I promise you, it will not be enough.

I cannot tell you how much danger the churches of America are in right now because they think they know how to function outside the presence of God. If God does not show up on a Sunday morning, our churches have mastered the art of faking it, of pretending God's manifested presence is among us, and continuing on with the meeting like it's no big deal.

Jesus did not say, "Apart from Me, you won't have very good meetings." In John 15:5, He said, "*I am the vine, you are the branches; he who abides in Me and I in him, he bears much fruit, for apart from Me you can do nothing.*" He wasn't kidding. This was not hyperbole. The reason Western society has not been changed by the power of God is because the Church has done a whole lot of nothing. We have pretended to love God's presence, but we have not taught our people the glorious joy of abiding in Jesus. It really is no wonder that we haven't seen much eternal fruit produced, because we think we can do life without the abiding presence of Jesus.

Saul did have the anointing, but he showed no desire for God's presence. He did not place a priority on having the presence of God with him. Saul never bothered to inquire of the Lord. When he realized that people were leaving him, he disobeyed God's instructions and moved ahead without God's presence or blessing. Even knowing that God was offended at him didn't bring him to repentance. He did not repent, but he still wanted Samuel to "worship" with him. The truth is this: Saul was not interested in seeking God; he was interested in looking like he was seeking God.

Our ministers and churches seem to love the King Saul method, but if you wholeheartedly pursue the Lord like David did, that will get you labeled as strange, even radical. It will even make King Saul throw a spear at you.

The more King Saul moved away from God and His presence and tried to do things in his own power, the more he felt the need to try to maintain the attention of the people of Israel. The drive to seek attention caused him to turn into a demonized, spear-throwing monster who was willing to ignore the needs of his people to stage a manhunt against an innocent man. Why was he so desperate for attention? Because he had made the critical mistake of assuming that authority and attention are the same thing. Nothing could be further from the truth!

We have an entire ministry culture that has been contaminating the Church. We think, "If I look good enough, if I can preach good enough, if I can lead worship good enough, they'll hand me the microphone." Friend, we must come to a place where we are seeking Jesus instead of seeking attention, or we will never be able to host His presence in our lives and churches! Oh, God, deliver us from this auditioning spirit!

What if you have been losing your spiritual authority because you have been auditioning for a ministry platform rather than pursuing God's presence? What if our churches and ministers look a lot more like Saul than David? What can we do about this?

David shows us the key to his entire life in one of his most famous psalms, Psalm 27. In verse four, David says, "*One thing I have asked from the Lord, that I shall seek: that I may dwell in the house of the Lord all the days of my life, to behold the beauty of the Lord and to meditate in His temple.*" In verse eight, he says,

"When You said, 'Seek My face,' my heart said to You, 'Your face, O Lord, I shall seek.'"

This is what set David apart. David knew that it was God who had established his kingship, his dynasty, and he wanted to honor the One who had brought him up from the shepherd field. David had the right idea. He had a hunger for God's presence, and he wanted to do something about that hunger. He was famous for inquiring of the Lord, and he was completely dedicated to hosting God.

This is what attracted God to David's life—this pervading passion to enjoy intimate fellowship with the Lord. It was the hallmark of David's life. If we are going to be a revival remnant, a people preoccupied with the presence of the Lord, then we must have the same hallmark. Fellowship with God must be our top priority.

David's hunger was good, but what he did about it was not. In his haste, he made a critical error.

Hasty hunger will always get you in trouble! David decided to move the Ark of the Covenant to Jerusalem, and that was a good decision. But he did not decide to consult the Word of God regarding how to bring the Ark to Jerusalem. He neglected to check the Torah for the protocol of carrying and entering God's presence. My friend, there is a protocol to entering the presence of the Lord.

One of the books that has helped me so much in learning to host the Lord is *Glory* by Ruth Ward Heflin. In that book, she said this: "You praise until the spirit of worship comes. You worship until the glory comes. Then, you stand in the glory." Many people seem to find this difficult, because this type of protocol will usually not fit into a twenty-minute package. This is not a fun, new way to put songs together; it is a protocol that surpasses music and gets down into your lifestyle. Haste is never involved in real worship, and when you allow yourself to make decisions in hasty hunger, you will always find yourself making serious errors.

There is a progression when you're hosting His presence! When you fail to follow the protocol, you won't consult God's instructions. Any time we fail to consult God's Word, disaster is the inevitable result.

You see, those who long for authentic revival find their joy in the presence of the Lord. Reading His Word is life to their souls. Worshiping before His Throne and enjoying His presence are not occasional activities; He has become their heartbeat. They are willing to pay the price of time to be with Jesus because they have found Him to be worth it.

Our churches have failed to press in for real revival because we care more about the clock on the wall than the Presence in the room. I am reminded of something C.S. Lewis once said: "Revival is not going to come until most of us really want it." The main reason we are not seeing a radical move of the Holy Spirit is because most of us think we have this church thing figured out without Him.

Let's take a momentary pause from the life of David to look at the last week of Jesus' time on earth. He specifically chose to spend the last few days of His life in the home of Lazarus, Mary, and Martha. I find that so interesting.

When I am going through something, I tend to gravitate toward my family. We are not perfect, but we certainly know how to circle the wagons when one of us is going through something. If I had been in Jesus' shoes, I would have gone home to Mary. Surely, when you're about to endure the worst thing anyone could ever go through, you go home to Mama. But that isn't what Jesus chose to do. He went to Lazarus's house.

Do you think that Jesus spent His last week of His natural life at Lazarus's house because it was close to Jerusalem, or could it be that they had learned how to host Him well? Could it be that they had mastered the art of taking care of His needs and making Him feel wanted? Could it be that they had learned how to make the King of Heaven feel comfortable in their home? I say again, Jesus comes and stays where He is hosted well.

In a moment of hasty hunger, David said, "Build me a new cart." David's hasty hunger had a death toll associated with it. The pitfall of hasty hunger is something that every revivalist must avoid.

Let me illustrate this. Nathan and I have some wonderful friends in Mississippi, Pastors Hardy and Jill Jones. They are salt of the earth kind of folks, and they invited Nathan and me to come and minister in their church. Nathan was flying in from another country, so I set off to meet him at the Jones' house in Mississippi.

One of the reasons I love Jill Jones is because that woman can cook like you would not believe. She used to own her own restaurant, and it shows. She says, "I'm going to go into the kitchen and throw something together." The things she "throws together" will throw you into fits of culinary delight. She is just unbelievable!

As I was making my way to Mississippi from Florida, I made a stop in Pensacola to use the restroom. I had been driving for several hours, not eating anything. I came out of the restroom to find a shelf fully stocked with massive bags of Cool Ranch Doritos. I was so tempted to grab a snack and go for it! I stood there for a few seconds debating with myself over whether or not I should do this. That's when I realized only a moron grabs a bag of Doritos when you can have a steak!

Eating a bag of chips will give you a sensation of fullness, but any nutritionist will tell you, those are empty calories. You made yourself feel full by grabbing a quick snack, but you have not nourished your body at all. Hasty hunger will settle for anything, but that is not good at all!

David's hasty hunger gave him a "new cart mentality." Where on earth did he get the idea to carry God's presence on a new cart? God never instructed anyone to carry the Ark on a cart. That idea came from the lost. The only other time in biblical history that the Ark was carried on a new cart was when the Philistines were sending it back to Israel after they had captured it in battle.

David's first experience as a warrior was when he faced Goliath, who was a Philistine. Yet when it was time to draw God's presence closer, when it was time to go deeper, he decided to pursue God in a way that he had learned from the very people he fought as a boy. They were his sworn enemies! Why was he trying to mimic their approach to God's presence?

Remember when David ran away to live in a Philistine city called Ziklag? God never told him to run away or to live his life outside of the covenant territory. In fact, as long as he stayed in the wilderness of Judea (praise), Saul couldn't so much as lay a hand on him. But the minute David moved in fear to the land of the Philistines, his city was attacked and he lost everything in a moment. Only when David became friendly with his enemy did he expose his life to attack.

Do we really need the nightclub laser-light smoke machine stuff in the house of God, or have we learned a new cart mentality? Do we really need to make our churches look like this world to win this world? We don't need mood music or mood lighting to experience the power of God. How much more truth must we sacrifice on the altar of relevance to win people to Jesus? We need deliverance from the Philistine approach!

You cannot do spiritual things in a worldly way and expect to get supernatural results. It doesn't work that way! The Word declares in Proverbs 3:5-6, "*Trust in the Lord with all your heart and do not lean on your own understanding. In all your ways acknowledge Him, and He will make your paths straight.*" We need to stop trying to figure out new methods and trust in the Lord once again. We need a return to reverence and to the Word.

Sincere desire for God's presence did not excuse the irreverence of David and Uzzah. That shows us that the moment we try to carry the presence of God without the fear of God, we have stepped outside the boundaries of His protection. We dare not make these same mistakes, lest we see similar results.

Uzzah's name means "strength." You see, when man's strength tries to bring natural stability to a move of God, it always ends in disaster. You can encourage a revival, you can speak into a move of God, but it must be done through the Word and through prayer. If you try to steady the movement of God's Spirit with the "wisdom" of man, you will find yourself becoming "seeker sensitive" instead of being "Spirit sensitive."

When you base your life on trying not to offend people, you will always find that the Holy Spirit is the One you become willing to offend. Somewhere along the way, we decided that the Holy Spirit was too "offensive" for the main sanctuary. We excused Him to a side room. Can you imagine telling the mighty Third Person of the Trinity that He is offensive? That He's too much for some people to take? That He no longer applies to today's world? Friend, we need the real Holy Spirit, not more meetings engineered to please people. God, have mercy on us!

God's presence was never meant to be carted around on something man-made. He wanted to be carried on the shoulders of His people who were called by His name. In the Torah, God instructed Moses to anoint the priests with oil and to mark them with the blood of the sacrifice (see Exodus 29). These anointed priests would minister to the Lord and to the people, and the consecrated Levites were to carry the Ark by poles that they would lift up onto their shoulders.

God never meant for His presence to be carted on a worldly method, but He wants to be hosted on the shoulders of the sanctified ones. Where are the called-out ones, the sanctified ones, the holy people? Where are the ones who pursue Him above all else? First Peter 2:9-10 says:

> *But you are a chosen race, a royal priesthood, a holy nation, a people for God's own possession, so that you may proclaim the excellencies of Him who has called you out of darkness into His marvelous light; for you once were not a people, but now you are the people of God; you had not received mercy, but now you have received mercy.*

God is looking for a sanctified, consecrated remnant. He's looking for those who have been marked by the blood of Jesus and anointed by His Spirit. The way you carry God's presence matters.

People say, "You can't have a service that lasts more than an hour and a half. You won't get people to come." Friend, what kind of people do you want in your church? Do you want people who will marinate in God's presence, or do you want McDonald's people who have to be talked into coming at all? Perhaps people have been bored with our churches because we told them they would meet the Lord, but they couldn't find Him among us.

The Ark was supposed to be carried by the anointed ones, not driven on a man-made method. We must return to the separation of real holiness. We must return to the preaching of the blood of Jesus. We must value the anointing of the Holy Spirit. These things are essential to the one who claims to want authentic revival.

When David returned to sacrifice and to the structure God had ordained, habitation became possible. It turns out that God and David both had the same thing in mind—they both wanted God to dwell. God wants to dwell, to tabernacle, to settle down among His people.

David had the priests escort the Ark of the Covenant back to Jerusalem, but every six steps he would stop the whole procession to offer sacrifices. This might have seemed extravagant to the outside perspective, but God just went ahead and received it because He knew that He deserved it.

Imagine a parade that moves that slowly. Imagine how much blood soaked the ground that day. But God saw that David had returned to His protocol, and He kissed it with His presence.

God's presence is meant to be carried or hosted by holy ones who make it their lives to serve Him. This cannot be a hobby; this has to be everyday life.

Would you take a moment to pray with me?

> *Father, I want to be a separated, consecrated, anointed one who carries Your presence in reverence and awe. By Your Spirit, please teach me how to host You well, in Jesus' name, amen.*

Chapter 8

SNAKE VOICES: THE NEED FOR DISCERNMENT

And this I pray, that your love may abound still more and more in real knowledge and all discernment, so that you may approve the things that are excellent, in order to be sincere and blameless until the day of Christ; having been filled with the fruit of righteousness which comes through Jesus Christ, to the glory and praise of God (Philippians 1:9-11).

A FEW YEARS AGO, I found myself watching a video on YouTube. Back in the good old days, you had to wonder what the crazy people were doing with their time. Now, thanks to modern technology, they will be happy to livestream it for you. And even though most people say that they find social media annoying, you can tell it's not true, because the view counts go off the charts!

I watched in horror as a lady set her phone on a tripod to record herself in the bathroom. She had filled up her bathtub with a great, big bubble bath, and she proceeded to hoist into the tub a massive, yellow, twelve-foot long Amazonian python. A python!

When I was growing up, Granddaddy taught me, "Honey, the only good snake is a dead snake, and even then I don't trust it." I could not believe that this lady was trusting this snake that could not only have killed her, but she would have suffered tremendously in the process. Anybody with sense should know you do not give a snake a bubble bath!

The comments were insane. People were telling her, "Lady, don't you understand that this thing could kill you? This is a predator!" But she ignored them all. I could hear her on the video talking to the snake, saying things like, "You are just too cute! You are all smelly. Let's get you into the bath!" And the snake propped its head up onto the side of the tub, hissing at her. The snake's head was easily the size of a bowling ball. I could not believe what I was seeing!

Why is it so disturbing to see a woman give a snake a bubble bath? It's because of this: you cannot treat a predator like it's a pet. Someone will get hurt!

Deception is one of the biggest predators that the twenty-first-century Church has ever faced, and it is running rampant. There is something wrong in the Church when we would rather make friends with the devil instead of casting him out. Something is amiss when we'd rather stroke our favorite sin instead of falling to our knees in repentance. The sin that we excuse from our pulpits will soon be celebrated in the streets of our nation. We need a return of Holy Ghost discernment in the Body of Christ!

We must decide today that we will no longer be seduced by the voice of the snake. We have to choose to listen to the real Holy Spirit, and we must never settle for anything less!

I want us to look at something that happened to the apostle Paul. Paul and his team were on their way to an open-air prayer meeting, but they were very rudely interrupted by a demon spirit.

> *It happened that as we were going to the place of prayer, a slave-girl having a spirit of divination met us, who was bringing her masters much profit by fortune-telling. Following after Paul and us, she kept crying out, saying, "These men are bond-servants of the Most High God, who are proclaiming to you the way of salvation." She continued doing this for many days. But Paul was greatly annoyed, and turned and said to the spirit, "I command you in the name of Jesus Christ to come out of her!" And it came out at that very moment* (Acts 16:16-18).

Friend, I understand that we are living in a society that loves to cancel everyone who is even remotely offensive. I know that pastors and preachers have been intimidated into stroking people's issues instead of following Paul's instructions to the Ephesians and "speaking the truth in love." But at some point, we are going to have to stop dancing around the issues and actually speak some biblical truth.

The Church must learn once again to treat a snake like a snake! If this story in the book of Acts was happening in today's church culture, we would have recommended this young lady to a counselor. We would have tried to talk her out of her problems, or we would have tried to pretend that nothing was wrong in the first place.

Please do not misunderstand me: not only do I love counseling in its proper context, but I have been on the receiving end of godly counsel. But you cannot talk a devil out no matter how you try.

When I was a little girl, we would frequently have people wander into our church off the streets. People would come in drunk, high, or both; and it was nothing in the world for Granddaddy and the prayer team to gather around that person and pray them through. They would cast the devil out of them, lead them to salvation in Jesus, and pray them through to the baptism of the Holy Spirit with the evidence of speaking in tongues.

What the old time Pentecostals had a prayer for, our modern churches have a chat for. I want you to talk to anyone you need to talk to. I see nothing wrong with that. But if the source of your problem is a demon, a chat is not going to make your problem go away. You need someone who can call a snake a snake!

Most people in our churches today would not have even recognized a problem with the young lady in Paul's meeting.

They would not have understood what was wrong with her message. She was shouting, "These men are servants of God! Listen to them!"

The problem was the source, because the source was a snake. The source was a spirit of darkness that was trying to manipulate the situation to its own benefit. We need to cry out to God to open up our eyes once again. When you're dealing with the devil, it's time to plead the blood of Jesus and get rid of the snake!

We need God to open our eyes once again. We need to know what we are looking at. We need to know those who labor among us. We have had so much deception in the Church, so many ministers who are deceivers. Friend, believe me, if you want a move of God in your life and in your church, you had better start crying out for discernment right now, because the enemy will come to deceive you.

In Matthew 24, the disciples instigated a conversation with Jesus that caused Him to start detailing the signs of the end times. He listed things like wars, rumors of wars, pestilence, famine, earthquakes in various places, and so on. I find it so disturbing that all of these signs of the times are in full play right now, but never in my lifetime has there been less preaching on the soon return of Jesus Christ than there is right now. Perhaps that's because the spirit of deception has been loosed in these last days.

Jesus only repeated one of the signs of the end times. Many of these signs are so extreme, but Jesus did not repeat earthquakes or pestilence. The only sign that He repeated, He actually repeated three times. It was this: "Let no one deceive you!" Friend, that is why I believe that the greatest distinction, the greatest sign that we are living in the last days, is that deception is not just out there in the world, but it has crept into our pulpits!

While the Church abandoned the altars of prayer, the enemy took that opportunity to spew out deception over our airways. When I was a little girl, you rarely ever heard of anyone who was struggling with same-sex attraction. I am thirty-eight at the time of this writing, and now we have preachers trying to reinvent the Bible to endorse the LGBTQ agenda. Years ago, preachers knew it was wrong to steal people's money to live lavish lifestyles in mansions, claiming those offerings went to the work of the Lord. Hardly anyone thinks anything of it now. Granddaddy's generation wouldn't understand why we think we can minister without spending time in prayer and Bible study, but we have our own little cute church Ted Talks now. They're laced with lousy versions of pop psychology, and what little Scripture is used in these "sermons" is so twisted, it is beyond recognition. Surely, we are in the last days!

One of the main deceptive plots of the enemy has been to normalize sin, not only to those outside the faith but to those who sit in our churches week after week. In the early days of the Pentecostal movement, those people believed in holiness. They read and studied the Word of God, and they believed everything in the Book. They would not go to movies. They wouldn't drink. They wouldn't play cards. They avoided the very appearance of evil.

Believe me when I tell you, I understand that while one generation lived in holiness, another generation was corrupted with legalism. But when we started allowing worldly influences into the Church, can you honestly tell me that it has helped us?

We have churches in the USA that start off their morning "worship" with secular music. I have done everything I know to do to understand that, but I just can't make it happen. Why are we mixing the holy with the profane? Why do we think that playing a Coldplay song before our service is going to make us appealing to the lost? Have we lost our minds?

Friend, it is not okay to listen to just any kind of music. This is why it is not okay to watch just anything on TV. This is why it matters what you allow in your family. The things you are streaming are having a profound effect on your spirituality, whether you're willing to admit that or not.

When deception becomes normal, you place yourself in a vulnerable position with the enemy.

The Greek word that is used for *fortune-telling* or *divination* is actually the same Greek word, *pythos*, from which we get the word *python*. Now, a python is a large, heavy-bodied snake that kills its victims by literally squeezing the life out of them.

How does a python kill its victim?

You must understand that the enemy wants to wrap himself around your life and begin to squeeze. He wants to constrict the flow of the breath of God in your life. Isn't it interesting that in Hebrew the Holy Spirit is called the *Ruach Ha Kodesh*, or the "Holy Breath of God"? No wonder the enemy has gone to such extraordinary means to keep you from receiving the power of the Holy Ghost. No wonder he has done everything in his power to keep the Spirit of God from moving in our churches. The deceptive python is wrapping itself around the Western Church, applying pressure and cutting off the airflow, the breath of God.

You might have said it this way: "I've just been going through so much that I'm finding it hard to sense God's presence." The devil wants to put pressure on you until you can't breathe. In fact, I promise you, the attack on your life is about seeing how much pressure the enemy can bring on you so that he can break you.

The next thing that the python does in its process of killing a victim is that he cuts off the circulation, keeping the blood from reaching vital points in the body.

I have never seen a time like we're living in today, when preachers are embarrassed and ashamed to preach about the precious blood of Jesus Christ. God never intended for His Church to be a self-help organization that made you feel better; rather, He intends to have a people who have been washed in the blood of Jesus, sanctified by His Spirit, and unashamed of His great sacrifice.

I have heard people say, "People don't understand when you talk about the blood of Jesus. It's too gory. You can't talk like that." Friend, you have got to be kidding me. The movies and shows that this generation watches on a daily basis are absolutely soaked in blood. They're not offended by blood, but they are offended by cowardice. Could it be that the real problem is that we have bought into the lies of the spirit of deception? Could it be that we need God to raise up some preachers of the blood like we have never seen before?

The final stage in a python attack is to crush your bone structure, making you easier to digest. Once you give in to that deceptive spirit of darkness, it is very difficult to break its power.

While we try to make friends with the devil and just try to keep the peace, the enemy is looking to totally crush you and devour you. This is not a negotiation! It's time to wake up!

In Greek times, Python was a serpent spirit located in the city of Delphi. This demon spirit of divination would possess someone, and they would speak "prophetically." They would release a word, and many times it would sound right. But the individual through whom this divination spirit would speak would not appear to even open their mouth. In fact, this is where we get our English word *ventriloquist*. It was an unholy utterance from an unholy source. It always sounded good, but it would wrap itself around you and put pressure on you.

You see, now Paul's response to this spirit of divination makes perfect sense. We read in Acts 16 that Paul and his team were on their way to an open-air prayer meeting, but because of what that demon shouted, we can safely assume that Paul was preaching Jesus. So when the young lady began to shout, "These men are servants of the Most High God; listen to them," we need to understand it in the context of this python spirit. That young lady was shouting without even opening her mouth. If you were in the group of people who were listening to Paul, don't you think you would be really distracted from hearing his message?

That's why Paul put a stop to it. Paul understood what we need to understand again: you cannot entertain the serpent and you must not listen to it! *You have to get rid of it! If the enemy can talk you into thinking that your pet sin is harmless, if he can deceive you in just one area of your life, he can cause a downward spiral that will take you lower than you ever thought you could go.*

We need to cry out for discernment, because we cannot afford to listen to the deception of the enemy!

You know, I have done all kinds of things in my life that have made people mad, but nothing has ever come close to when we named our firstborn son "Malachi David." I can't tell you how many people got upset that Nathan and I used that name. Everyone we met had an opinion about it. But the Lord had spoken that name to us, so we would not be moved.

Actually, the Lord woke me up one morning, back in 2008. I had not even met my husband yet, and I was not dating anyone. The Lord woke me up out of a sound sleep and said, "Your first son will be Malachi David!"

I tried to politely remind God that I wasn't seeing anyone at the time, let alone married and ready for a son. I said, "God, I think You forgot something."

He said, "Nevertheless, your first son will be Malachi David." From that time on, I would call Malachi's name in prayer.

Because of my son's name, I began to study the book of Malachi. You know, the name means, "My messenger." It is truly amazing what this prophet of God had to say in the book that bears his name. I'm not sure if you know it or not, but there is quite a lot more in there than just tithing. This prophet had much to say that we should be listening to.

The book of Malachi, chapter 4, speaks of the revival that we are all believing God for. It's the revival in which the hearts of the fathers turn to the hearts of the sons and the sons to their fathers. We need this so desperately in the USA, where most of the horrific school shootings we have seen have happened at the hands of fatherless sons. We need revival that breaks through the pandemic of fatherlessness!

Before you get to Malachi 4, we read this verse in chapter 3:18, *"So you will again distinguish between the righteous and the wicked, between one who serves God and one who does not serve Him."*

My friend, if we want a Malachi 4 revival, we must begin to cry out for a Malachi 3 discernment! We must have God open up our spiritual eyes. We need to cry out for the Holy Spirit, the Spirit of wisdom and revelation, to come upon the Church once again.

Most people probably know the story of Samson, but for those of you who don't, you can find it in the book of Judges. That is some hard-core reading. If you would read the book of Judges, you could just cancel your subscription to Netflix. It would certainly be rated for a mature audience.

Samson was called before his birth to live his life as a Nazirite. It was a vow of extreme holiness and consecration. He would never drink or eat so much as a grape. The outward marking of this extreme holiness was his long hair. The Nazirite vow prevented him from being allowed to cut his hair. Every time people saw Samson, they would think of that holiness.

Now, when I talk about Samson, a lot of people would probably think about a not-so-green version of the Incredible Hulk. People tend to think that Samson was some kind of muscle-bound, 400-pound massive guy. I do not believe that. That just doesn't make sense with the story.

For one thing, people were all the time asking him, "What is the secret of your strength?" If the guy is 400 pounds and ripped, the secret of his strength is not a mystery; it is steroids! Nobody asks someone who looks like that what their secret is.

But if Samson was only a little guy, if he only weighed about 100 pounds, if he looked a whole lot like Barney Fife (from *The Andy Griffith Show*) with dreadlocks, that is going to provoke some people to ask where he gets his strength. If some wimpy guy takes the jawbone of a donkey and kills a thousand trained Philistine warriors, you have to know this guy is getting his strength from a supernatural source.

I checked Samson's story in the book of Judges, and it turns out that he never once exercised strength outside of this phrase: "The Spirit of the Lord came upon Samson." And if that's not enough evidence for you, a haircut doesn't usually come with symptoms of extreme weakness. The source of Samson's strength was the Spirit of God.

Samson got involved with a woman he had no business being with. Her name was Delilah, and she was a Philistine. The Law of God strictly forbade Israelite men from intermarrying with Gentile women, unless that woman came into covenant with God, abiding by His Law. Delilah had done no such thing. Samson was having a relationship with this woman that he knew was wrong, but he deceived himself into thinking it was okay for him to do it.

How many ministers have preached against sexual sin while carrying on extramarital affairs themselves, deceiving themselves into thinking that what was wrong for others was acceptable for them?

The Philistines came to Delilah and hired her to find out the secret of Samson's strength. She was being paid well to spend time with him. Samson was the thorn in the side of the Philistines; you might even say that he was like a most-wanted terrorist to them. God had used him to hold the Philistines at bay, preventing them from taking Israel's territory, but he became so seduced by the spirit of deception that he found himself in Delilah's bed.

Delilah asked him, *"What is the secret of your strength?"* The first several times, he made up ridiculous answers. On the first night she asked that, he responded, *"If they bind me with seven fresh cords that have not been dried, I will become weak and be like any other man."* So she did it. Delilah bound him with the cords, then she shouted, *"Samson, the Philistines are upon you!"* She had hidden them in an inner room of her house. They came to attack Samson, but he snapped the cords and they could not touch him.

If you want to know whether or not Samson was dealing with deception, the next night, he was right back in her bed! He gave another fake answer, and the whole scenario played out again. He kept coming back to Delilah even though he was 100 percent sure she was working with his enemies. He knew she did not love him. But that deceptive spirit had so bound him, he couldn't stop coming back.

On the last night of this charade, Delilah really turned on the tears. She said, "If you really loved me, you would tell me your real secret. You don't really love me!" And that's when Samson told her about his Nazirite vow. That man was so deceived that even though he knew Delilah was totally corrupt, he still told her the truth—the secret of his strength.

And that is how Samson came to have his first haircut. Delilah let him get to sleep, and she cut his hair. When she shouted, "*The Philistines are upon you*," the Bible records that Samson got up and shook himself as before, "*but he did not know that the Lord had departed from him*" (Judges 16:20). Those are some of the saddest words in Scripture, but that is the nightmare that you can expect when you allow yourself to be deceived.

Then, we find this sad ending in Judges 16:21: "*Then the Philistines seized him and gouged out his eyes; and they brought him down to Gaza and bound him with bronze chains, and he was a grinder in the prison.*" This man who had been a mighty judge of Israel had been reduced to slavery in a prison because he opened up his life to deception.

When I read that Scripture, I started asking some questions. Why did the Philistines gouge out Samson's eyes? Why didn't they just kill him? If they hated him that much, if he was that big of an enemy, why not just take him out? And that's when it all came together.

The enemy was not after Samson's strength; *he was after his sight!* The devil knows what most of us seem to have forgotten—any strength, anything good, anything awesome that has happened in our lives is because of the Holy Spirit. But if the enemy can steal your sight, your vision, your discernment, you are as good as dead! Proverbs 29:18 says that without a vision the people perish!

We have to cry out to God for discernment to return to His people! We must be able to distinguish between the voice of God and the voice of the serpent! When the enemy speaks, he seldom comes right out with an anti-God message. He introduces subtle differences, little changes to what God has said. He has been doing that since the Garden of Eden.

It is so crucial in these last days that we not only judge what is spoken, but that we discern the source of what is spoken. Whose spirit is speaking right now? Are we hearing from the Holy Spirit, or are we hearing from a wrong spirit? The devil is the father of lies, but he will sometimes twist the truth. One of my teachers at Bible school used to say, "The only time the devil ever tells the truth is to make a lie bigger."

Here's what that would look like in a practical way:

- "You are lonely, and it's not good for you to be alone. You can date that guy. It doesn't matter that he isn't as passionate for God as you are. You can help him get there."
- "It's okay for you to only pay your tithes once in a while. I mean, God doesn't really need your money, and He understands that you have to look out for yourself."
- "God wants you to be happy. Surely, you can just sleep with whoever you want to."
- "It's okay for you to talk about that person's problems. You're trying to solve their problem, so it's not like you mean it in a bad way."

All of those statements hold a little kernel of truth, but every one of them twists it to the advantage of the enemy. Do you know the voice of the real Holy Spirit?

In John 10:27, Jesus said, "*My sheep hear My voice, and I know them, and they follow Me*"; but the number-one prayer request we get as we travel is for clarity in hearing the voice of God. The Church has been filling herself up with so many distractions and deceptions, we struggle to hear the voice of the Shepherd. This ought not to be.

The Holy Spirit only *ever* points to Jesus Christ! You see, in our account from Acts 16, the biggest problem with the message of this spirit of divination is that it pointed directly to Paul and Silas. She said, "*These men* are servants of the Most High God. Listen *to them*." That spirit was calling attention to the men of God instead of to God Himself. If you're not paying close attention to the message, you can easily miss it.

The Holy Spirit does not call attention to man. He always directly points to Jesus Christ, and He leaves no room to question that. He never comes to endorse any of our ministries. He does not come to improve our social media footprint or to give us a better stage presence. May it never be! The Holy Spirit always speaks of Jesus, and we know that because Jesus told us all about the job description of the Holy Spirit. Let's take a look at some of those passages.

> *But the Helper, the Holy Spirit, whom the Father will send in My name, He will teach you all things, and bring to your remembrance all that I said to you* (John 14:26).
>
> *When the Helper comes, whom I will send to you from the Father, that is the Spirit of truth who proceeds from the Father, He will testify about Me, and you will testify also, because you have been with Me from the beginning* (John 15:26-27).

The Holy Spirit testifies about Jesus, and when He comes on your life, you will testify of Jesus! Let me say it like this: I am an old-school Pentecostal. I still believe that the initial, physical evidence of the baptism of the Holy Spirit is speaking in tongues. I love speaking in tongues, and if you have not yet had that experience with God, I pray that He will baptize you even now, while you're reading this book.

But Jesus is saying here that the continual, ongoing evidence of the baptism of the Holy Spirit is that you cannot find a way to shut up about Him! My friend, if you have a Jesus that you have found a way to keep quiet about, you do not have the Jesus of the New Testament! When you really meet the Holy Spirit, what flows out of you is this: "Behold the Lamb of God who takes away the sin of the world!"

> *But I tell you the truth, it is to your advantage that I go away; for if I do not go away, the Helper will not come to you; but if I go, I will send Him to you. And He, when He comes, will convict the world concerning sin and righteousness and judgment; concerning sin, because they do not believe in Me; and concerning righteousness, because I go to the Father and you no longer see Me; and concerning judgment, because the ruler of this world has been judged* (John 16:7-11).

When the real Holy Ghost shows up, the message is always Jesus Christ! The trademark of the Holy Spirit is the truth about Jesus Christ. The Holy Spirit is the Spirit of Truth, so He will always point directly to the One who said, "I AM the truth!"

We could say it like this: the Holy Spirit is in the business of making Christ obvious in our lives. If you get a word that does not obviously point to Christ, you should instantly be suspicious of the source. If something is going on in a service that does not glorify Jesus but puts the emphasis on man, you should be concerned.

When I saw these Scriptures and my own need for discernment, I began to pray a simple prayer, the kind of prayer that has the power to drastically change a life: "Holy Spirit, make Jesus obvious in my life." I had no idea what would come of praying that prayer, or I might never have prayed it.

When I asked Holy Spirit to make Jesus obvious, I meant, "When I lead worship, I want You to come. When I preach, I want You to arrest hearts. When I pray for people, I want You to heal them." There's nothing wrong with any of that, except I had the work of the Holy Spirit completely categorized to church ministry. I'm so glad that when God births a prayer in my spirit, He answers it according to His intentions, not mine!

The "answers" to that prayer came on a day that I did not even feel spiritual. I was jet-lagged from a recent trip to Malaysia. We were in Georgia to recover from our trip and to pick Malachi up (this was before Jeremiah was born). I don't know how to describe trans-Pacific jet lag, but I will say this: there is not a cup of coffee big enough to fix it. Nathan and I were exhausted.

We had to stop by a place of business in Augusta. Nathan said to me, "You're gonna have a word for that lady." She was the owner of the business. I had never met her before, this certainly was not an altar call, and I did not have a word at all.

We went in, and after exchanging pleasantries with the lady, it got kind of quiet. She was getting on with her work, and I felt awkward, because I had not gotten a word for her. Nathan always knows when I'm about to get a word, so I have learned not to argue with him, but I just couldn't help but feel weird about all this. Not out loud, but in my spirit, I said, "Lord, our time is almost up here. If You want me to give this young lady a word, I'm gonna need You to go ahead and give it. I'm not going to make anything up."

The moment I prayed that, the lady looked at me, and right out of nowhere, she started confessing her sins. In a matter of about thirty seconds, she confessed to sleeping with three different men, getting drunk, and partying. But she said, "I know God has a call on my life. I know I'm supposed to preach the Gospel, but I also know that I'm going to have to get my life right and stop all this before I get behind a pulpit."

I was flabbergasted! I never expected all of that to come out of this woman. Keep in mind, she didn't even know me, and she was confessing major sin to a perfect stranger. I told her, "Honey, you know better than to live like that. You must not get behind a pulpit and preach until you get your life right with God. The Bible tells us that those who teach and preach will be held to a higher level of accountability before God. If you get up to preach with active sin in your life like that, you're liable to bring the wrath of God on yourself." You see, Nathan was right—I did have a word for her.

That same day, we went to the mall to get the battery replaced in Nathan's watch. The guy behind the counter immediately started to confess how much he liked to go to nightclubs and get completely drunk, dancing on the tabletops. Again, we did not know the man and he did not know that we were preachers.

I looked at Nathan and said, "What is up with this day? What is going on right now? Why is everyone confessing their sins to me?"

And the Lord reminded me, "You asked Me for this."

You see, the Holy Spirit, the Spirit of Truth, wants to make Jesus obvious in your home, your job, your school, and wherever else you have a voice of influence. He wants to set you free from deception and walk you into the powerful truth of who Jesus really is. Will you let Him do that?

Let's pray that prayer, and I want you to pray it with all your heart. Get ready for what the answer will look like!

> *Holy Spirit, make Jesus obvious in my life! Break every chain of deception, and let me walk in Your truth and in Holy Ghost discernment, in Jesus' name, amen.*

Chapter 9

IT'S TIME TO SHAKE IT UP!

But about midnight Paul and Silas were praying and singing hymns of praise to God, and the prisoners were listening to them; and suddenly there came a great earthquake, so that the foundations of the prison house were shaken; and immediately all the doors were opened and everyone's chains were unfastened (Acts 16:25-26).

IN THE LAST CHAPTER, we took a look at the moment when Paul cast the spirit of divination out of the young slave girl. I'm sure we could all agree that that was an intense moment. Right in the middle of Paul and Silas preaching, the demon in that young lady was manifesting and drawing attention to itself, thus distracting from the preaching about Jesus.

Demons love to do that. They love to try to interrupt in the middle of a move of God, because they're hoping that you will start paying attention to them instead of what Jesus is doing. Distraction is one of the biggest plays in the devil's playbook, and he uses it frequently in a revival setting. He does not want the message of the Gospel to gain momentum. He wants to shut it all down as quickly as possible.

As we travel, deliverance is something we deal with from time to time, but it's hard to reconcile what happened to Paul and Silas with my own experience. When I have had to cast out a demon, I have noticed that most of the churches we go to will respond with great celebration. We all start rejoicing because Jesus has brought freedom to someone who was held captive by demonic bondage. We throw a praise party, and we pray for the Holy Spirit to fill the recently freed person with His presence. I don't think I have ever seen anyone get angry at us because someone got delivered. It's hard to imagine it, but that is exactly what happened in Acts 16.

Paul and Silas got in trouble for doing something right. I'm not sure where we got the idea that every time the Lord uses us, everyone is going to congratulate us. We have become so addicted to the approval of man that we expect affirmation every time we do the right thing. Paul and Silas certainly didn't experience that. Instead of praising God for the young lady's freedom, the crowd brought in the police and told them that Paul and Silas were troublemakers bent on starting a riot.

The attack of the enemy against these men of God shows us a strategy that hell uses still today to derail a revival coming to a city. If the enemy can't tempt the ministry leadership to fall into sin, you can expect an attack similar to what Paul and Silas experienced. You may not be happy to hear that, but I feel the urgency of telling you the truth. The path to revival is not an easy one, and the devil will not ignore you. If you pursue revival through prayer and determine in your heart not to compromise the truth of the Gospel, you will paint a target on your life.

I once saw a comic cartoon called *The Far Side*. In it, two deer were standing around and talking. One of them had what appeared to be a massive target covering his body. His deer buddy looked at him and said, "Bummer of a birth mark, Hal."

Friend, when you decide that you are going to press in for a move of God that looks like the book of Acts, you might as well look yourself in the mirror and say, "Bummer of a birthmark." You have a target on your back, and the enemy is coming for you. The good news is that we serve the undefeated God, the Mighty Warrior Himself, and He always takes care of His own. But Paul said, "We are not ignorant of the devil's schemes." We need to be aware of what's coming.

The first thing that happened in this attack against Paul and Silas is that the soldiers stripped the robes off their backs. This was humiliating and degrading. This is what the enemy seeks to do in a revival—he wants to take the mantle of authority right off your back, bringing mockery against you.

We are in a time right now when the enemy is coming against the mantle of authority in such a vicious way. You can be anything as long as you're not anointed. You can have a ministry, you can have a website, you can even livestream every week; but don't you dare preach with authority. The moment you step into the mantle that God ordained for your life, you can expect hell to contest it. To put on a mantle is to step into the arena of warfare.

One of the greatest threats against the kingdom of darkness is the Church rising up, empowered to do the works of the ministry by the fivefold ministry. Apostles, prophets, pastors, teachers, and evangelists are mantled by God to equip the Body of Christ. Let me remind you that the fivefold ministry is functional. You don't get to strut with a brand-new, fancy title. But those who flow in the function of the fivefold scare the living daylights out of the devil, because he knows that where the fivefold functions in unity and humility, the Church will begin to experience New Testament revival and results.

That is why he targets the mantle. He wants to strip it off of you and make you wonder if you were ever called in the first place. Friend, if you can be intimidated, you will be. You need to ask the Holy Spirit to give you a boldness that will not buckle under pressure. Do not concede the mantle God has given you. Do not surrender even an inch of territory.

The second thing the soldiers did to Paul and Silas after stripping them of their robes was no better than the first—they beat their backs with rods. Now, there was pain involved. Keep in mind, all these men did was preach Jesus and get a young lady delivered. They were now suffering for that.

When I was pregnant with my second son, Jeremiah Nathan, he decided that it would be a lot of fun to spend most of the pregnancy dancing on my sciatic nerve. The pain was incredible. I talked to my doctor and I talked to a physical therapist, but nothing we did could get that boy to stop dancing on that nerve. I would preach with him doing dance moves the whole time, sending shock waves of pain throughout my body. Needless to say, I was one happy Mama when he was born and no longer had access to that nerve.

There really is nothing quite like back pain. Anyone who has ever experienced it can testify—if you have back pain, you have big pain. It affects everything. It limits you, and it can be totally debilitating. That's why the enemy selects this particular strategy.

The back represents your stability, your core, your very foundation. If the enemy can beat you down in the foundational elements of your life and ministry, he can stop your progress in what God has called you to do. He loves to attack the structure of who you are. If he can't pressure you to fall into sin, he will strike out at your fundamental identity in Christ, making you wonder if who you are is wrong. His objective is to send you in a cycle of introspection, questioning your calling, your gifts, the anointing on your life, and everyone around you. This kind of introspection is not healthy at all. It makes you take your eyes off of Jesus and put them onto yourself. It makes you want to take the attack personally, when it's actually not even about you in the first place.

Allow me to help you right now. This is something that I have not always gotten right, so I could truthfully say that this is a lesson I have had to learn the hard way. I am begging you—do not make the mistake of taking the attack personally.

Paul and Silas could have when they were stripped and beaten, you know. They could have gotten offended. They were hurting. They were wounded. They could have been angry at the people who turned them in. They could have been mad at the Roman soldiers. But you see, the real issue was not that one young lady or this one mob riot.

God had opened up a door of ministry for Paul and Silas in the region of Macedonia, and this whole attack was about the enemy pushing back on that door and saying, "You are not coming in here! This is my territory!"

If I could get you to stop taking everything so personally and zoom out, I could get your focus back where it belongs. It's not the people you're ministering to who are mad at you; it's that the enemy does not want you to take the territory God has assigned for your life. It's not that people are not receiving your ministry; it's that the enemy feels the threat of the Kingdom of Heaven advancing in a region. Don't get offended and don't take it personally. Something more is happening to you than what you understand right now.

The final stage of the attack was that the soldiers confined Paul and Silas to prison. They did not just imprison Paul and Silas; they were put into the inner prison and their feet were put into stocks. I looked it up, and the inner prison was a place that was used for torture. Roman stocks were not just designed to keep you from moving, but also to function as a way to cause greater strains and ruptures to the body. It is totally conceivable that in addition to having been beaten with rods, Paul and Silas were quite possibly being prepared for further torture.

What makes this sort of punishment the devil's weapon of choice against Paul and Silas? Why did the enemy not just beat them and throw them into a cell? Why did he want them to be put into the stocks? Why did the enemy care where their feet were? When I started asking these questions, I believe the Holy Spirit dropped the answer into my spirit. The Bible says in Deuteronomy 11:24:

> *Every place on which the sole of your foot treads shall be yours; your border will be from the wilderness to Lebanon, and from the river, the river Euphrates, as far as the western sea.*

I understand that God was speaking to Israel through Moses, but I believe there is a principle here that applies to those of us who have been grafted in through the New Covenant. We must understand that everywhere we go, God wants us to possess that territory for His Kingdom. Jesus did not save us so that we could be passive believers; He has called us to bring His kingdom to every location He has assigned us to.

The enemy did not just want to beat Paul and Silas or embarrass them. He did not just want to confine them. He wanted their feet off of his territory! As long as their feet were on the ground, the kingdom of darkness was in danger. He wanted to immobilize so that the Kingdom of God would make no more forward progress.

Friend, let me be the one to tell you—the devil wants your feet off of his territory! This is why you must zoom out and see the big picture. The attack was never about Paul and Silas as individuals; it was about stopping the message of the Gospel from going forth. It was about keeping a region locked down in bondage to the enemy. This is why Isaiah 52:7 says:

> *How lovely on the mountains are the feet of him who brings good news, who announces peace and brings good news of happiness, who announces salvation, and says to Zion, "Your God reigns!"*

You have got to start taking the attack as a compliment. You stepped into the devil's territory and you made him nervous. It's hard to remember that when you're the one who has been immobilized by an unforeseen attack. It's difficult to stay focused when it feels like you have had the daylights beaten out of you or when you have been publicly humiliated. It's hard to function in joy when the enemy is coming after your family. But you must remember, hell would not respond with such violence and aggression if they didn't feel like you were a threat.

Matthew 11:12 says, *"From the days of John the Baptist until now the kingdom of heaven suffers violence, and violent men take it by force."* The attack of the enemy is violent, and when the people of God stand and contend for revival in a region, you better believe that hell sees that as an act of aggression.

How are you going to respond to the violence? We must stop agreeing to the terms and conditions of the attack of the enemy. We have to stop treating a temporary attack like it's a permanent condition. When the enemy is forbidding you to move forward, you have a choice as to how you are going to respond.

Paul and Silas responded by transforming the place of their confinement into a place of consecration. One thing I love about walking with Jesus is this: you can turn just about any place into an altar! You can take the place where they slandered you and make it an altar. You can take the place where people tried to come against your family and make it an altar. You can take the place where you were hurt or abused or ostracized and you can turn it into a point of contact with Heaven!

When you make an altar out of the stones that the devil throws at your life, you rob him of the power of discouraging you. When you build an altar, you dethrone the enemy and you enthrone the Lord in His rightful place. You can whine about your situation, but that will not bring about change. When you turn your situation into an opportunity to praise the Lord, you yank the rug right out from under the devil.

You must learn to praise God from the place you did not choose. You may not have chosen the situation you're facing, but you can choose to respond in praise. You see, God always revealed aspects of His divine nature by releasing His name situationally. For instance, Abraham would never have known the Lord our Provider had he not had to lay down his son on an altar as a sacrifice. Israel would never have known God as the Deliverer had they not been in bondage. They would never have known Jehovah Rapha had there not been a lot of sick people walking through the wilderness. David would never have known God as the Lord of the Breakthrough had he not been fighting a very real enemy. God reveals Himself situationally! Maybe you didn't choose your situation, but if you will praise God from the place you did not choose, you had better get ready, because He is about to reveal Himself to you in a way you have never known Him before! We serve the God who never wastes a situation. You have the privilege of partnering with Heaven to shift your circumstance.

Paul and Silas demonstrated a golden key: they chose to intermingle their prayer with their praise. The combination of prayer and praise is the biblically prescribed recipe for breakthrough! Cindy Jacobs once said, "If we are to pray without ceasing and we are to let the high praises of God continually be in our mouth, then praise is prayer and prayer is praise." Prayer and praise are two branches off the same tree. When we combine our prayer with our praise, that is when we see the breakthrough come.

We all have gone through terrible seasons of attack, seasons when we could not see breakthrough a mile away. We have all gone through seemingly hopeless situations, seasons of intense satanic attack. But I want to suggest to you that if you will build an altar of prayer and praise in your life, you can shift your season. You can break the enemy's power to confine you and constrain you. You can set your feet back down on the territory God has assigned you to, and the enemy will not be able to stop you!

One of my favorite ways to combine prayer and praise in my own life is something I like to call "Opposite Mode." Whatever the enemy is coming against me with, I will praise God with the direct opposite. For example, if the enemy is attacking my health, I take that opportunity to lift my voice and say, "Jesus, You are Jehovah Rapha, the Lord my Healer, and I give You praise!" If the devil is coming against our ministry, I say, "Lord, You are the Lord of Hosts, the Mighty Warrior, and You have never lost a battle. I give You praise!" If the enemy is fighting us financially, my response is always, "Jesus, Your name is Jehovah

Jireh, the God who sees my need and provides for it. I give You praise because You have always been faithful to me!"

Maybe the situation you are facing right now is horrific. Maybe you have never gone through anything worse. Maybe you feel like there is nowhere for you to turn. Maybe you feel beaten and confined by the enemy. I want you to know the solution to the shifting of your season is in your vocal cords. Your breakthrough is in your mouth. You see, when you praise God for who He is, and when you begin to pray His identity over your situation in the opposite to what the enemy is doing, something powerful happens. Your praise and your prayer combine to form a prophetic declaration that if God has ever done it before, He is about to do it again. When I choose to remember aloud the great faithfulness of the Lord, my situation has to bow to who He is!

At the sound of Paul and Silas' prayer and praise combined, the substructure of the prison house began to shake, causing their chains to fall off and the prison doors to swing wide open. You see, your prayer and your praise combine to birth a sudden move of God in your life! Do you want to know what Heaven is waiting for? Heaven is listening in for your praise. When you release it, the ancient foundational structures that hell designed to lock you down are going to shake you right out of that attack. They're going to be forced not just to let you go, but to break the chains off of everyone around you who has been confined by the enemy.

When you press through to your breakthrough, it is going to have a profound effect on your family, your church, your ministry, and everyone you have influence over. The other prisoners were listening to Paul and Silas as they praised. You have no idea the impact your praise could be having. In the middle of the horrible situations that the USA and the international community are facing, your lost friends and loved ones are listening for your voice. Are you going to agree with the terms and conditions of the attack of the enemy, or are you going to let your praise on earth agree with the praise in Heaven?

The proper response to the attack of the enemy is to release your prayer and praise until you shake the substructure of hell. It's time for you to open up your mouth, because that high praise you're releasing is going to release something supernatural! You know, a natural earthquake would not have only shaken the prison house. It wouldn't have made chains fall off. This was a supernatural shaking that rode in on the sound of deep prayer and high praise. We need a supernatural shaking that has both internal and external results! What if God began to shake things on the inside until the chains fell off on the outside? It's time to shake it up!

Their praise and prayer birthed a shaking, and the shaking broke their lockdown. When they were escorted out of the prison, the sign that they had begun to take territory for the Kingdom was that the jailer and his entire household got saved and baptized in the middle of the night. Paul and Silas did not give an altar call; the jailer saw what their praise produced and was immediately ready to bow to the superior power of Jesus Christ.

We are crossing over into a season when the fish are going to jump into the boat. You may not need a new soul-winning strategy. You just need to release a fresh prayer, a high praise, and watch it shift your region for the glory of God.

I lived in Daphne, Alabama, for about seven years while I served at Church of His Presence. When I moved to the area, I learned about a phenomenon that happens on the shores of the Mobile Bay from time to time. They call it a Jubilee; in fact, Daphne is called "The Jubilee City." No one knows exactly why this happens, but occasionally, certain types of fish and crabs will swim to the shores of the Mobile Bay and jump out of the water. Marine biologists do not understand why it happens, but they can see the migration of the fish happening. They report it on the local news, telling the locals, "We are having a Jubilee, so get your bucket and go to the shore."

You see, any other time of the year, you would have to actually fish to catch something. But during a Jubilee, what you would normally have to work for will just jump right out of the water.

Could I prophesy to you right now? My friend, as you release your prayer and your praise, I speak over your life: it is time to get your bucket! What God is about to release over your life is going to cause your lost family members and loved ones to jump right out of the waters of sin and depravity and right into the bucket of God's amazing grace. You had better get ready to see your children come home. Get ready to see God restore finances that the devil stole from you. Get ready to get your marriage back. Get ready to see your region shaken by the power and glory of God.

In the name of Jesus, it is time to shake it up!

Pray with me:

> *Father, I ask You to protect my heart from offense in the midst of the attack of the enemy. I ask You*

to give me the boldness to combine my prayer with my praise, that I might see the Kingdom of God advance in the territory You have assigned me to, in Jesus' name, amen.

Chapter 10

THE UNLIKELY ONES

Because the foolishness of God is wiser than men, and the weakness of God is stronger than men. For consider your calling, brethren, that there were not many wise according to the flesh, not many mighty, not many noble; but God has chosen the foolish things of the world to shame the wise, and God has chosen the weak things of the world to shame the things which are strong, and the base things of the world and the despised God has chosen, the things that are not, so that He may nullify the things that are, so that no man may boast before God. But by His doing you are in Christ Jesus, who became to us wisdom from God, and righteousness and sanctification, and redemption, so that, just as it is written, "Let him who boasts, boast in the Lord" (1 Corinthians 1:25-31).

OUR GOD TAKES GREAT delight in using people whom no one else would ever dream of using. He does it so that there will never be any danger of us appropriating the glory that is only due to His name. These are the last days, and in these last days He is looking for a remnant people who are willing to believe God for more than just their own life, but who are willing to rise up under the power and demonstration of the Holy Ghost to shift entire regions for His glory. We need some people who are willing to do more than just live a normal life. We need some real revivalists who are going to see the Kingdom of God advance!

God is coming for the people who got passed over on the first round. He's coming to use people who do not have their life together, who do not feel ready for what He wants them to do. God wants to use some people who are aware of their own shortcomings and limitations. He wants to use people who have been counted out because of their past. He wants to use people whose family does not even believe they are called. Let me tell you in the name of Jesus, He is coming for the unlikely ones!

Our God is determined to choose the people who are the least likely to succeed. This is not something He does by accident; He selects the weakest people on purpose. Everyone you can think of who has been used by God in a powerful way has dealt with extraordinary weakness. God likes it that way!

You see, God intentionally chose Moses. This was a man who had killed someone so that everyone would know he was called to be a deliverer. He acted out in his own strength. He became a fugitive, and then he spent forty years of his life as a shepherd in the middle of nowhere. When God called to Moses from the burning bush, Moses tried to talk God out of using him. He had all kinds of reasons why God should not have chosen him, and get this—he wasn't wrong! But God took that man, called him, and made him to be the deliverer of Israel. God used a murderer as a deliverer, causing Moses to walk the children of Israel out of slavery and oppression and into inheritance and sonship. God is coming for the unlikely ones!

God knows how to use Jacob the con man, the schemer, the supplanter, the deceiver. Jacob never approached anybody without having an angle. He defended himself at all costs. He promoted himself even when it cost him his relationship with his immediate family. He always had a scheme going! God got a hold of that boy and wrestled with him. The Bible says that God touched the socket of Jacob's hip, and he walked differently for the rest of his life. The Lord put a new name on Jacob, and in one moment he went from being Jacob the Schemer to being Israel, the Prince of God. God birthed His chosen nation out of that broken, messed-up life, because God is coming for the unlikely ones!

The infinitely merciful God that we serve chose to rescue a prostitute named Rahab. What I love about God is this: God did not just spare her life and save her family in the battle of Jericho and let her become a part of the nation of Israel. I mean, that would have been more than enough by anyone's standard. She got an entirely new life because God rescued her, but He did not just stop there. Our God so thoroughly chose that former prostitute that you can find Rahab's name in the genealogy of Jesus Christ the Son of God! That is the nature of our God. He is over the top, and He chooses the people whom no one else would ever give a second chance to. He's coming for the unlikely ones!

God chose the prophet Elijah. This man was a redneck by all standards. He spent a significant portion of his ministry camping outside instead of sleeping indoors. He was not a man who could claim to have any people skills. He was not nice. If Elijah came to your church to preach, you would probably find him highly offensive. He called out sin so directly that most people simply could not handle him. God took that wild man and put such a mantle on his life than in one day, in one altar call, an entire nation came to repentance, saying, "The Lord, He is God!" You would never have thought it to look at Elijah, but God used that man to pray a whole nation through. I'm telling you, God always chooses the unlikely ones!

God chose a little punk shepherd boy named David. There was nothing remarkable about his life; I mean, the only way he got to fight Goliath in the first place was because he had delivered a pizza to his brothers who were on the battlefield. I say it was pizza because the Bible says that it was bread and cheese. This was happening in the region of the Mediterranean; you cannot tell me that there was no sauce. David was just a pizza delivery guy whose other job was tending sheep for his father. He had not come of age yet. He was not a mature leader. He was not battle-tested.

By the way, David's father, Jesse, did not like David very much at all. If you'll remember, when Samuel the prophet came to Jesse's house to anoint the next king of Israel, neither Jesse nor anyone else in his household even thought it was a good idea to invite David to that church service. Samuel had to stop the whole thing and tell Jesse, "Send for your other son. Bring him out of that shepherd's field. We won't even sit down until he gets here." Can you imagine how awkward that must have been for the rest of the family who didn't think David could possibly be in the lineup for the throne of Israel? If there has ever been an awkward moment in Scripture, it has to be David's family waiting around for him to come in from the pasture, feeling ridiculous for not believing that he should have been there in the first place.

David was selected by God because he had been out in the fields singing love songs to his God. God took that little shepherd boy who smelled too much like the sheep and called him out, anointed him, and put him on the throne of Israel. God used David's life to teach generations of people to say, "The Lord is my shepherd; I shall not want!" Who could have been more unlikely than this shepherd king?

Oh, let that give you hope for your teenage children right now. I don't care how messed up they are. I don't care how unqualified you think they are. If God can use David, God can use your sons and daughters! They may be out partying right now. They may think that you are too stupid to live because you pray for them in the Holy Ghost. They may be making your life a living hell; but the more unqualified they are, the more you will find them being targeted by the Holy Spirit to be used in the Kingdom of God. Hallelujah!

God chose Peter, who was an absolute coward. That guy chickened out on Jesus three times, as if once was not enough. Judas betrayed Jesus only once; Peter did it three times! The only real difference was that he wept bitter tears of repentance. Before Jesus went to the Cross, Peter only really got it right two times. The rest of the time, it's hard not to cringe when you read the things this man said and did. He was a loud mouth and a hot head. He was an accident waiting to happen.

Right after Peter released the great confession, "You are the Christ, the Son of the Living God," he blew it worse than he ever had before. Jesus was telling the disciples that He was going to suffer and die on the Cross, and Peter stepped up to the plate. Peter told Jesus, "It's not going to happen. We won't let it happen. You are not going to suffer and die." In that moment, Peter was echoing the devil himself! If your concept of Jesus is all nice all the time, imagine what it would have been like to witness this particular conversation. Jesus looked Peter in the eye and said, "Get behind me, satan!"

Wow! I have heard some rebukes in my time, but I have never been called the devil! It really cannot get a lot worse than that.

But God got ahold of Peter's life. He took a man who was all bark and no bite, saved him, and filled him with the Holy Ghost. Peter was such a changed man that on the Day of Pentecost it was he who God used to define the parameters of what we call revival and outpouring today. Surely, we serve the God who chooses the unlikely ones!

God chose the most stuck-up, arrogant, religious scholar he could find, a man by the name of Saul of Tarsus. He was a violent persecutor of the early Church. He was dragging followers of Jesus off to prison and certain death. He thought he was doing God a favor!

In one moment, God knocked Saul right off his donkey and shone the light of Heaven in his eyes; Jesus personally confronted him. Saul let go of everything he thought he knew to embrace his Messiah, and he ended up going by the name Paul.

God used this violent hater of Jesus the Messiah to stand up and proclaim, "I am not ashamed of the Gospel of Jesus Christ, for it is the power of God unto salvation, to the Jew first and also to the Greek."

I don't know about you, but I am so glad that our God loves to use the unlikely ones!

I hope you will hear my heart on this, but I want you to know that God is not looking for the next big preacher. He's not looking for the next great prophetic voice or the next up-and-coming worship leader. God is not looking for the polished people; He is looking for those who know that they do not have it all together. He is looking for the ones who know that they are not qualified and that they are in desperate need of Him! God is no longer taking auditions for ministry platforms. We already have more than enough attention-seekers claiming to speak for Heaven.

God is looking to use a remnant of people who have not bowed their knee to the false narcissistic gospel that is being preached in the Western world. You may say, "Lydia, what are you talking about?"

I'm talking about this false message that has been going around that says that Jesus died to give you a destiny. This thing where we have become so concerned about our own destiny and our own calling all the time. It sounds so good and I'm sure it's well-intentioned, but it is false and narcissistic. How do I know that? Because if your eyes are on you and your calling and your destiny, they are not on Jesus Christ.

The Gospel is not that Jesus came to give you purpose; it is that Jesus bled, died, and rose again to catch you up into calling! We have been caught up into the hope of His calling, according to His inheritance, and we have been called up into His destiny. Allow me to remind you that the destiny of Jesus can be found in Philippians chapter 2, where it says that at the name of Jesus, every knee shall bow and every tongue shall confess that He is Lord, to the glory of God the Father. Whether you realize it or not, friend, everything really is all about Jesus! For from Him are all things, and to Him are all things. If you will worship the Lord with your whole life and do the Great Commission, you will not miss your destiny because you will be so fascinated with the destiny of Jesus.

God is looking for those who have learned the glory of total dependence on the Person of Jesus Christ. I have to say that because so many people are still so dependent on certain worship leaders or specific preachers. God is looking for the people who are not propping up their prayer life through some other person, but instead they are looking only to Jesus by His Spirit. You see, friend, when you lean your whole life on the Person of Jesus, Heaven calls you "usable." When you resist that, God will let you sit on the bench for a while until you humble yourself and admit your need for Him.

Did you know that when we try to act like we don't need the Lord, when we try to polish up our ministries and strut, that is actually repulsive to the Holy Spirit? When we try to polish up our services, we do that to appeal to people. The moment you did that, you broke the first commandment. "You shall love the Lord your God, and *Him only* shall you serve." Why is the Holy Spirit not really moving in churches that look like nightclubs? It's because they are trying to serve the wrong crowd. They're trying to serve earth, when Heaven should have been their objective.

One of the most unlikely candidates God ever selected was Gideon, so I want us to take a look at his story. Nobody would have ever chosen him. Gideon was a coward. He liked to argue with God. He was not the important person in his tribe, and his tribe held no great significance. Yet God selected him and used him to bring about a great victory for Israel.

> *Then the sons of Israel did what was evil in the sight of the Lord; and the Lord gave them into the hands of Midian seven years. The power of Midian prevailed against Israel. Because of Midian the sons of Israel made for themselves the dens which were in the mountains and the caves and the strongholds. For it was when Israel had sown, that the Midianites would come up with the Amalekites and the sons of the east and go against them. So they would camp against them and destroy the produce of the earth as far as Gaza, and leave no sustenance in Israel as well as no sheep, ox, or donkey. For they would come up with their livestock and their tents, they would come in like locusts for number, both they and their camels were innumerable; and they came into the land to devastate it. So Israel was brought very low because of Midian, and the sons of Israel cried to the Lord* (Judges 6:1-6).

I want you to notice with me that Israel was in a totally backslidden condition. It's not that they did not know God; they were in a covenant with Him! But they had chosen to step out on Him by worshiping other gods, and the Lord called it spiritual adultery. This is what it means to be backslidden; there was a covenant in place, but it was being mocked.

The backslidden condition of Israel meant that the economic and political fight that they were facing was happening completely because they had walked away from the Lord. As it was then, so it is today. If you look at the condition of the United States and the other nations of the Western world, you can easily see the condition of the Church's prayer life. If you have a problem with where your nation is headed, you're going to need to do more than go to the polls, although you should do that. We could never have seen such wickedness and corruption, especially in the USA, if the Church had actually been praying like it should have been. The problems we are facing are far more than political; they are spiritual, and they require a supernatural solution.

The more backslidden Israel became, we find that they built strongholds for themselves. How do you end up dealing with strongholds? We build strongholds when we have drifted from the Lord, the enemy comes to oppress us, and instead of repenting and crying out to God, we bow.

You know, everyone has dealt with strongholds in their life at some point or another. Everybody's got junk in their family line. I know what it's like to get set free from strongholds and generational curses in my own life. I can't fault anyone for having a struggle, but what bothers me is when you find someone making themselves comfortable in their stronghold. You should not be decorating your stronghold, picking out carpet and wallpaper and settling down there. The problem I have is when the people of God defend their junk instead of bringing it to the altar to be washed away in the blood of Jesus! We have an entire generation of people who would rather receive attention for their strongholds instead of getting free, but I believe that the tide is turning.

If you say the word *deliverance*, people in church culture get so weird so fast. They get very afraid, and they want to take it to a back room. I understand that some people have gotten biblically out of line with deliverance, and I will not go along with that. But I believe in deliverance for this reason: the next generation of mighty warriors is hiding out in their strongholds, totally bound by the lies of the enemy, and at some point somebody has to go get them! It's time for you to go after your lost loved ones and say, "In Jesus' name, you are coming out of your darkness and into His marvelous light!" Friend, you had better start believing in deliverance, because we serve the God who comes to set the captives free!

I want to make myself totally clear: God is looking for the ones who are crack addicts. God is looking for the folks in the gay bars. God is looking for the ones who are so bound by witchcraft and religion. God is looking for the unlikely ones!

> *Then the angel of the Lord came and sat under the oak that was in Ophrah, which belonged to Joash the Abiezrite as his son Gideon was beating out wheat in the wine press in order to save it from the Midianites. The angel of the Lord appeared to him and said to him, "The Lord is with you, O valiant warrior." Then Gideon said to him, "O my lord, if the Lord is with us, why then has all this happened to us? And where are all His miracles which our fathers told us about, saying, 'Did*

> *not the Lord bring us up from Egypt?' But now the Lord has abandoned us and given us into the hand of Midian." The Lord looked at him and said, "Go in this your strength and deliver Israel from the hand of Midian. Have I not sent you?" He said to Him, "O Lord, how shall I deliver Israel? Behold, my family is the least in Manasseh, and I am the youngest in my father's house." But the Lord said to him, "Surely I will be with you, and you shall defeat Midian as one man"* (Judges 6:11-16).

What God did for Gideon here was astonishing. Many theologians believe that Gideon was experiencing something that they call a theophany, which was an appearance of Jesus Christ before He was born of a virgin in Bethlehem. This is one of my favorite things about Jesus! I love that He was so eager to interfere with the affairs of mankind that some things just could not wait until Bethlehem. He loves us so much!

Gideon was surely experiencing the encounter of a lifetime! I'm sure any of us would love to have the opportunity to sit down with the Lord face to face, having the privilege of asking Him specific questions and getting precise answers about our lives. Think about this: the God of the universe was hanging out under the tree in Gideon's backyard! What an unspeakable demonstration of the favor of God!

When I read the conversation that Gideon had with God, I just want to shake the guy. He was sitting there straight up arguing with Jesus! I want to say, "Gideon, you have the opportunity to talk to God about anything you want. Ask Him about some of the tough theological questions that everyone trips over. Ask Him about what He wants for your nation. Ask God anything you want to, but stop arguing!" But I find it difficult to remain frustrated with the way Gideon argued with God when I remember my own prayer life.

I want you to notice that God ignored Gideon's insecure, argumentative accusations against His nature. Why? Friend, God did not answer Gideon according to his insecurity because it was not relevant. When you accuse God and call it prayer, God will not answer that. In fact, many people become frustrated with the Lord because they don't think He is answering their prayers, when in reality they're not praying; they're accusing God and calling it prayer.

God's response to Gideon's insecurity was to call Gideon back up into His plan for his life. Even though Gideon himself didn't understand what God was saying, God kept calling him up higher. You see, this is one of the reasons God calls the unlikely ones—He would rather minister to your insecurity than to have to smack down your pride.

The unlikely ones have a hard time seeing in themselves what God sees in them, but that is why God delights in choosing them. They know better than to take the credit for themselves. They know if anything good comes from their life, it's God.

Part of the reason why you are afraid of moving from seeking out your own destiny and instead stepping into God's eternal story is because you think God is depending on you. Oh, can I tell you, that is not the case! He is depending on His own Spirit on the inside of you to accomplish His purpose for your life. Your job is to yield, to surrender completely to Him, and let Him lead you into His destiny!

I looked up the meaning of Gideon's name, and this is what I found: "feller; cutter down; one who cuts down; a hewer down; a cutting down; he that bruises; great warrior."

Would you look at that? If you take a closer look at Judges 6, you will realize that Gideon's father, Joash, did not serve the Lord. That man was completely backslidden, and he was an idol worshiper, but that man chose a name that prophesied what his son would accomplish for God. It was in Gideon's name the whole time! Let's look at what happened next.

> *Now on the same night the Lord said to him, "Take your father's bull and a second bull seven years old, and pull down the altar of Baal which belongs to your father, and cut down the Asherah that is beside it; and build an altar to the Lord your God on the top of this stronghold in an orderly manner, and take a second bull and offer a burnt offering with the wood of the Asherah which you shall cut down." Then Gideon took ten men of his servants and did as the Lord had spoken to him; and because he was too afraid of his father's household and the men of the city to do it by day, he did it by night. When the men of the city arose early in the morning, behold, the altar of Baal was torn down, and the Asherah which was beside it was cut down, and the second bull was offered on the altar which had been built* (Judges 6:25-28).

Let me tell you something about the unlikely ones—they worship differently. They don't stay bound to generational curses that have plagued their family for several generations. They take a very aggressive stance toward that which is false, and they bring back the family altar!

Please believe me when I tell you that the season we are in requires us to restore the family altar in our homes. We must become people of prayer, not just in our churches but in our homes. You see, Gideon had to pull down the false worship in his family and reestablish the worship of Yahweh in his family before God could use his life. Friend, the key to your next season is in your living room, not just in the sanctuary of your own home.

God is looking for some unlikely people to stand up and say, "This satanic junk is not going to run in my family anymore. The spirit of infirmity is not going to limit my family anymore. This false worship is not going to run in my family anymore. It stops right here and it stops right now!" It's time for some mighty warriors to stand up and use their worship to fight their way through to freedom!

God refused to use Gideon's life until the false gods had been torn down. When Gideon's family woke up in the morning, they saw the destruction of that system of false religion. I speak over your life in the name of Jesus that your family is about to wake up to find all the fake stuff burned down. They're going to see a restored family altar in your house. The curse is broken in the mighty name of Jesus!

Once Gideon got the worship issue settled, he began to rally the people to fight against Midian. Right from the start, God started culling the warriors by saying, "Tell them that anyone who is afraid is free to go back home." The Word tells us that thousands of fighters turned around and did just that.

Imagine how Gideon must have felt, watching those men leave their provisions and walk away from the fight! He may have wanted to join them.

I have found that when you become a pursuer of revival, many people will rise up and pass the fear test, but only a tiny remnant can pass the water test.

> *So he brought the people down to the water. And the Lord said to Gideon, "You shall separate everyone who laps the water with his tongue as a dog laps, as well as everyone who kneels to drink." Now the number of those who lapped, putting their hand to their mouth, was 300 men; but all the rest of the people kneeled to drink water. The Lord said to Gideon, "I will deliver you with the 300 men who lapped and will give the Midianites into your hands; so let all the other people go, each man to his home"* (Judges 7:5-7).

The unlikely ones drink from the river of God just a little bit differently.

You see, God could only use the ones who got all the way down, completely low to the ground. The ones who drank on their knees with their face in the water and their rear end in the air were actually making themselves a target of the enemy. They were a danger to everyone around them, because they drank the water in a way that showed they were only concerned about themselves.

I am all about you drinking from the river of God, but you must learn how to do it in humility, with your whole life lowered before the Lord. God cannot use you if you still have your rear end in the air! You will endanger yourself and everyone in your life if you try to pursue revival in a self-centered way.

Only the ones who were all the way down could drink while keeping their eyes open for their enemy. That is because the Bible does not just instruct us to pray; it says, "Watch and pray!"

Pursuing revival is not just about you, it's about everyone your life is supposed to touch for the Kingdom. It's about your brothers and sisters in Christ who are fighting beside you. You must drink from the river, but you must keep your eyes open for the attack of the enemy. You must not allow yourself to be seduced by selfishness.

The next thing that happened in Gideon's story is so interesting to me. The Bible tells us that God invited Gideon to go and spy on the camp of the Midianites, assuring him that what he would overhear would silence any remaining fears that he had. Gideon took his servant and went straight to the camp, so we know that Gideon must have needed some extra reassurance before he moved forward.

Don't you love the fact that God did not work Gideon over for that? At this point, I would probably have been frustrated with Gideon's fear, but God continued to call him up higher to a place of faith. God extends that same kindness to us, friend. He will go to great lengths to call you out of fear and into faith.

When Gideon approached the Midianite camp, this is what he overheard:

> *When Gideon came, behold, a man was relating a dream to his friend. And he said, "Behold, I had a dream; a loaf of barley bread was tumbling into the camp of Midian, and it came to the tent and struck*

> *it so that it fell, and turned it upside down so that the tent lay flat." His friend replied, "This is nothing less than the sword of Gideon the son of Joash, a man of Israel; God has given Midian and all the camp into his hand"* (Judges 7:13-14).

Let me tell you something about the unlikely ones—they listen just a little bit differently. They don't treat prayer like it's a one-way communication, with them just venting to God. The unlikely ones have learned how to listen in prayer, to hear God's voice, and for God to show them what the enemy is saying about them.

Are you listening? Are you hearing what God wants you to hear about your enemy?

What Gideon heard at that camp caused him to rise up in courage from that moment on. The dream that the Midianite man had was a powerful prophecy of the victory Israel was about to win.

The loaf of barley bread symbolized Israel, of course, but I believe it was also a picture of the Bread of Presence destroying the enemy's camp.

I know that so many people like to talk about how we need to gain a strategy to defeat the works of darkness in our day. But I believe that the greatest strategy we could have as a remnant of end-time revivalists is to become a people who are obsessed with the Bread of God's presence. When Jesus is exalted and His presence draws near, He steps in to fight the battle for us. The Bible still says, "Let God arise and His enemies be scattered!" And let us not forget that Jesus said, "I am the bread that came down from Heaven." We must be people of the

Presence, because that will forever be the highest strategy for spiritual warfare.

I want us to take a look at how the Gideon's battle unfolded.

> *So Gideon and the hundred men who were with him came to the outskirts of the camp at the beginning of the middle watch, when they had just posted the watch; and they blew the trumpets and smashed the pitchers that were in their hands. When the three companies blew the trumpets and broke the pitchers, they held the torches in their left hands and the trumpets in their right hands for blowing, and cried, "A sword for the Lord and for Gideon!" Each stood in his place around the camp; and all the army ran, crying out as they fled. When they blew 300 trumpets, the Lord set the sword of one against another even throughout the whole army; and the army fled as far as Beth-shittah toward Zererah, as far as the edge of Abel-meholah, by Tabbath* (Judges 7:19-22).

What a battle plan this was! If you were to try really hard, it would be difficult to come up with a plan that could possibly be more strange than this. In the natural, this plan just does not make sense. You see, the unlikely ones fight differently. This battle plan makes no sense unless you're paying attention to what was happening in the supernatural realm.

First, you have to understand that the fight begins with brokenness. It always does! God is going to use people in these last days in direct proportion to their level of brokenness. If you want God to use you, stay broken, stay teachable, and stay humble before Him. Your will must stay surrendered and your heart must remain soft.

Second, you need to raise up the torch. The light of God's revelation is going to uncover and expose every hidden thing the enemy has tried to accomplish against you. God is releasing the spirit of wisdom and revelation in the knowledge of God. As you lift up the great Light of the world, the light that radiates from Him is going to pierce the darkness around you. Light defeats darkness every single time. Don't ever forget that.

Third, Gideon's army sounded the trumpet. This is always the sound of an alarm that invites you to look at Jesus. In Revelation 1, John turned to see the voice that had been speaking with him, and he saw Jesus Himself. The sounding of the trumpet is the picture of us echoing the voice of Jesus to our generation. This is why I say that we need more Jesus in our preaching, in our praying, and in our conversation. When you focus your attention on Him alone, you will make it a practice to say what He says.

Finally, they shouted, "A sword for the Lord and for Gideon!" I believe that this was an invitation to the hosts of angelic armies to fight with and for Gideon's 300 men. There is simply no other explanation for how the armies of Midian were defeated. God wrought a great victory that day, and Gideon went from being a coward to a celebrated hero.

The victory in these last days will go to the unlikely ones, to those who believe what God has said about them and obey Him completely, no matter what the cost.

I invite you right now—come out of your strongholds. Come out of your insecurity. Grab a torch and a trumpet, and let's run to the fight. Will you pray with me?

> *Father, I ask You to fill every insecure place in my life with Your courage, Your Spirit. Help me to look past my own lack of qualifications and give me the strength to take You at Your Word, in Jesus' name, amen.*

Chapter 11

HAVING A FEARLESS HEART

Have I not commanded you? Be strong and courageous! Do not tremble or be dismayed, for the Lord your God is with you wherever you go (Joshua 1:9).

IN THE FIRST CHAPTER, I briefly shared about how I used to be paralyzed with fear. I remember hiding behind the pews in our church when I was a little girl because I was so afraid that someone in my family would make me get up in front of people. I wanted nothing to do with anything on a platform, and I told my whole family that. I just could not do it.

I remember one time when Mom desperately wanted me to sing a duet with her in church. She might as well have wanted me to walk on water for how terrified I was. We would practice at the house, but even at home I was sick to think about having to stand in front of people. I could not imagine anything more frightening.

The Sunday finally came, and there was nothing I could do to stop this thing from happening. I can remember walking up to the platform with Mom and holding the microphone and looking out at the congregation. My heart sank. It didn't seem to matter how prepared I was. Nothing was calming this fear in my heart.

Mom thought that I had decided not to sing. She thought I was lip syncing. She could not understand why I would work so hard to prepare and then fake my part of the duet. Here's the thing: I was singing as loud as I could, but I couldn't get any distinguishable sound to come out because I was so petrified. I'm not sure I have ever faced a more embarrassing moment in my life. I knew that I could sing that song, but I was totally unable to make it happen because of fear.

I know what it is to deal with paralyzing fear. The example I just gave was unfortunately only one of many, some of which did not involve ministry. I was a captive to fear, and it had a grip on my life.

When I met Jesus Christ in the altars of the Brownsville Revival in 1996, He completely changed me. Nobody asked the Lord to take fear away, but in the weeks following our encounter with God in revival, I found that all the fear was gone, and in its place was a boldness that I had never experienced before.

There are people reading this book right now who are dealing with fear and anxiety so badly that your life and calling has been extremely limited. I want you to know that when you encounter God in revival, you are not just going to experience good services; you are going to be freer than you have ever been in your life!

About a month after our first Brownsville experience of March 1996, we went to the Brownsville Pastor's Conference. Let me remind you, I was nearly twelve years old at the time. The church had a separate ministry time set up for the kids, and Mom asked if I wanted to go to that. I said, "Not a chance. There's no way I'm going to miss what the Holy Spirit is doing with all the grown-ups. It's not going to happen." I'm so glad she let me stay!

The power of God in those meetings was so raw, so unfiltered! We had never before heard people worship Jesus so intimately, like they really knew the Person they were singing to. We were overwhelmed with the presence and glory of God, and it felt like we were becoming saturated in the Holy Spirit.

On our way back to Augusta, things started getting a bit interesting. We had taken the church van, filling it with the church staff, primarily. But Grandmama, Dad's little Pentecostal mama, was also in that van.

Grandmama had had a wonderful time at Brownsville. She said, "This is just like old-time Pentecost!" We watched her run the pews, dance in the aisles, weep tears of joy, and encounter the Lord in a fresh way. She would say, "This is just the way I believe it!" And her eyes would just shine with the glory of God.

That night in the van, Grandmama said, "I think we ought to pray, and I think Lydia ought to lead us in prayer."

I immediately said, "No, I don't think so." I was not yet used to being set free. I responded the way I had always responded, because I didn't fully realize that the fear was gone.

Dad looked at me and said, "Your grandmother says you should pray, so you are going to pray." Thank God for old-school parents!

What happened next is hard to fully explain, but I will try. I remember saying, "Dear Jesus, we thank You for this day..." and then the fire of God fell in that ugly church van! It was like something exploded in me that had been bubbling up just below the surface. I felt like I was having an out-of-body experience. I heard myself saying, "And in the mighty name of Jesus, we claim the city of Augusta for the glory of God! We command every stronghold to fall right now, and we speak revival to our church and to our city!" The folks in the van begin to weep and wail. Some were experiencing holy laughter. The guy who was driving was swerving all over the road, and I could hear him praying in the Spirit. People were shaking uncontrollably, crying out to God fervently. That church van had become a rolling prayer meeting before any of us could even process what had happened.

There has never been any looking back. When the Lord broke that fear off of my life, He did it so thoroughly. I have never been the same. The boldness that I preach with is a direct result of the power of God to set the captives free, and I will be eternally grateful.

I believe that breakthrough is real when you cannot even find the traces of what you used to be bound by. As I minister throughout the United States and all over the world, people are shocked to find that there was ever a time that I was filled with fear. Let me tell you, that is not because I am such a great person of faith. This is just how good God is at setting people free. This is why the Bible says, "Whom the Son sets free is free indeed!" When Jesus set me free, I went from being filled with fear to having a fearless heart so fast that it took my head a while to catch up.

If you had told me that the day would come when I would preach to large crowds, I would have laughed in your face. If you had told me that I would lead worship in a major revival, going on to lead worship in the nations, I would have thought you were completely crazy. But when God infuses your life with the courage that can only come from His Holy Spirit, nothing in hell can stop you from fulfilling the purpose of God on your life.

There is an inner strength that speaks louder than the voice of the enemy. There is a fortitude that does not come from your personality or your upbringing. There is a tenacity that could only come from Heaven standing up on the inside, and everything good that has happened in my life has come because God gave me this courage. In and of myself, I would still be hiding behind a pew, but with the Holy Spirit, I am not afraid.

Webster's Dictionary from 1812 says this about courage: "COURAGE, noun [Latin, the heart.] Bravery; intrepidity; that quality of mind which enables men to encounter danger and difficulties with firmness, or without fear or depression of spirits; valor; boldness; resolution." In the 1812 edition of his dictionary, Noah Webster always cited a Bible reference for his definitions. The one he selected for courage was this: "Be strong and of good courage" (Deuteronomy 31:6).

I do not believe that courage is for those we might think are special, more anointed, more gifted, or more extroverted. I believe that the days we are living in demand that every child of God rise up with a heart full of courage to bravely live out what God has called us to do. We cannot afford to have anyone on the bench. These are the last of the last days, and we need every believer living at maximum capacity for the glory of God!

With all my heart, I believe that this courage that God gives is for everyone. It's for those of us who do not feel qualified. It's for those who don't feel ready to face a fight. It's for those who feel that someone else should take a stand.

A.W. Tozer said this: "A scared world needs a fearless church." Please allow that to sink in! Have you seen the news lately? The common denominator in every political story, every natural disaster, and every local event is fear. Everyone is afraid of something. Peace is a priceless commodity. And in the midst of that turmoil in the world, I am astonished to find that fear and anxiety have spread throughout the Body of Christ like a malignant cancer. It's as though we have forgotten that we serve the God who said, "*Behold, I am the Lord, the God of all flesh; is anything too difficult for Me?*" (Jeremiah 32:27).

God is not confused. He is not stressed out. Y'all, He is not even nervous. He knows who He is and He is confident in what He is capable of. If His children would ever catch a glimpse of His greatness, I am convinced that we would actually start believing and living like no weapon that is formed against us will prosper.

I believe that it is possible to live a courageous Christian life. I do not believe that we have to accept every attack of the enemy. I do not believe that we have to live in defeat and anxiety. We do not have to cower down in the corner while the enemy wreaks havoc in this generation. I believe that we can rise up in Holy Ghost boldness to represent the victorious Christ to this lost and dying world.

If you are going to step out of passive Christianity and start contending for revival in your region, you are going to need a courage that comes from the supernatural realm. God is so ready to pour it out!

I want us to look at a specific moment in the life of David. David has always been one of my personal heroes. I mean, when you have been a worship leader for a large portion of your life, you really have to have a certain appreciation for David, right? For years now, I have tried to go through his life story at least once a year. I am inspired by David's strengths, but I am also encouraged at how God used him in spite of his weaknesses and mistakes.

There are some striking elements to David's life. He is probably most famous for being a worshiper and a psalmist. His nation described him as the "sweet psalmist of Israel." He is also well known for having been Israel's greatest king. In the book of Acts, he is called a prophet. I find that so very interesting, because the Messiah came through David's lineage, but as a type of Christ, David also was a prophet, a priest, and a king. Wow! Those are the good things he was known for, but I am so glad that Scripture makes it clear that David did not always have his act together. He was an "all or nothing" kind of guy. When he failed, he failed massively. God did not have a special relationship with David because of David's perfection. David learned the art of repenting well, and that is what saved him.

But as I read about David's life, I am most intrigued by his great courage. This man was a warrior even before he knew how to fight. He fought the battles of the Lord with such fierceness that his enemies trembled at the sound of his name.

For me, there is no greater illustration of raw courage than the battle between David and Goliath. Most commentaries seem to suggest that David would have been a teenager at the time of this conflict. Goliath would have been somewhere between nine and thirteen feet tall.

In fact, Goliath would have been a sight to behold. This giant was a champion warrior. The Bible details his armor, and we find that not only was he decked out in some very impressive defensive wear, but he had a shield-bearer in front of him. That means that Goliath had both hands free for the fight. He was a formidable enemy, and he struck terror into the hearts of the Israelites and King Saul.

Picture this with me: you are David, stepping out into the valley of Elah where the battle is going to take place. Israel is on one hill, and the Philistines are on the opposite hill. The armies of Israel had no confidence in David, so it is hard to believe that they would be cheering him on. I imagine that the Philistines thought that with Goliath as their champion, there was simply no way they could lose. So you are David, you are standing on the battle line in this valley (which is where all battle lines are drawn), and you are facing this massive warrior all on your own. And you know that no one expects anything other than your death.

The amazing thing is that no one was making David fight this giant. If you read 1 Samuel 17, you will see that everyone was desperately trying to talk him out of fighting Goliath. No one thought he was able to do it. David did not have to go looking for reasons he wouldn't win the fight, because everyone around him was supplying those reasons for him. He was not qualified. He was too young. Goliath was too big. Goliath was an experienced warrior, and David had never even fought in a battle. His own brother even questioned his motives for wanting to fight. David could not even count on the support of his own family!

How did David have the audacity to fight this giant? How do you face something so completely impossible with the kind of courage David had?

You see, David had learned something that every one of us must understand: *courage is not about who you are; it's about who you have been with.*

When I was a teenager, I was on fire for God when a lot of my friends were not. If you add to that the fact that I have always been a bit of a nerd, well, that makes for an awkward adolescence. Suffice it to say that I would not have won any popularity contests.

Dad was not just the associate pastor at our church; he was also my youth pastor. I was the worship leader for the youth group, which is not an easy job when the majority of the group is only there because their parents made them come. They had decided that they wanted to live like the world and coming to church did not fit into their idea of being cool. But Dad preached Jesus, holiness, grace, and God's love, and he would not compromise the truth. I was proud of him.

One night, Dad had preached about holiness. Holiness is kind of a big deal, because the Bible says that without it, you cannot see God. Dad preached that you had to live right with the help of the Holy Spirit, that you could not have one foot in the world and one foot in the church. It was a good message, but it was not well received.

The youth group always met up at the foosball (table soccer) tables after church to have a little fun. We were all ridiculously good at foosball, so it was always a good time. That night, my brother, Philip, was my goalie and I was the striker. We were doing pretty good playing against a couple of older guys from the group. They were around seventeen and eighteen years old, and these guys were pretty big for their age. I was about sixteen, so Phil was about to turn twelve. He was still just a little kid.

You also have to understand that I have always been the outgoing one. Phil says that I am crazy. That boy was born calm, cool, and collected. He is always chilled out. Not that night.

The guys were saying that they could not believe Dad had preached the way he did. They were saying things like, "Why does he have to make such a big deal about everything? It's ridiculous! It's okay to have a little fun. Nobody wants to hear all that."

Well, I was getting upset, but before I could say anything, Phil spoke up. He said, "If you would get the sin out of your life, you wouldn't have to get upset when my Dad preaches about holiness." Talk about a "mic drop" moment! I was impressed.

But those other guys didn't take it so well. They started taunting my brother. They told him how stupid he was and that it wasn't his place to say anything to them. Then they really crossed the line. "We'll take you out back and teach you how to talk to us."

Right about then was when I felt the nuclear meltdown begin to occur. I felt the red in my hair come on, and before I could go and pray about it, I heard myself shout, "I dare you to touch him. If you so much as lay a fingernail on my brother, I will pick him up by the ankles and beat you with him. And then we are gonna let this whole church know that you two idiots got beat up by a girl!"

They backed off so fast! It was over before it could even get started. You know, Phil never had to lift a finger to defend himself that night, because he knew that someone in the room was well able to fight his battle for him.

You see, friend, David had the courage to face Goliath because he knew that someone on that battlefield was greater than he was! He knew that this battle was the Lord's and that our God is well capable of fighting for us!

When you truly start to understand the Scripture that says, "*Greater is He who is in you than he who is in the world*" (1 John 4:4), you will run quickly to the impossible battle that you face. What man calls impossible is actually effortless for our God! God has never wasted even a single second of time being intimidated by the devil. No way!

The difference between David and King Saul could not have been more apparent. Here we have King Saul, who had been anointed by God to rule over Israel, but who had removed himself from God's favor through his disobedience.

Oh, I know that we all want the favor of God, but please allow me to pause here for a moment. First, let me say to my brothers and sisters in the Western world that the favor of God is not something you can give an offering to obtain. God's favor is priceless! No matter who has told you differently, you cannot give an offering to win God's favor or any of the rest of His blessings. We either believe that Jesus paid it all, or we don't. We cannot give money to buy something that Jesus died on the Cross to give us. That is just nonsense.

The favor of God goes to those who obey Him to what others might call an extreme. He kisses the lives of those who put Him first, even when everyone else thinks that they're just going too far.

You see, Saul had started off so well. He was God's choice to be Israel's first king, and the Bible tells us that God's Spirit came upon him. He fought the enemies of God and was initially successful, but pride came into his heart. He even set up a monument to himself! The man who came to the throne of Israel feeling small and insignificant had become full of arrogance. When pride comes in, disobedience is inevitable. Saul heard the instructions of God through Samuel to utterly destroy the Amalekites and all their possessions, and outwardly he responded positively. He knew how to put on a good show! But he thought that he had a better idea than God. He chose to keep the king and all the "good stuff." When the prophet came to the battlefield, Saul suddenly knew what it was like to be removed from God's favor. Disobedience will remove you from the place of your destiny.

But David, no one even thought about as being chosen by God; this young man was not seeking God to win His favor. He was not seeking a position of power. David was a young man who had been assigned to shepherd his father's sheep, and he did it well. While he was in the fields with the sheep, he spent his time learning to minister to the Lord. He would write songs to the Lord and pour out his heart. He was no hotshot. He had no reason to be impressed with himself, and he certainly didn't have any encouragement from his family. All he knew was that he wanted God more than anything else in life, and it caused God to pay attention to him.

If there is one thing that I have learned, it is this: if you want God to back you up in the public place, you must learn to seek Him in the secret place! We've got to come to a place where we are far more concerned about ministering to the Lord than we are about seeking the approval of people. God is not looking for the next hotshot minister. He is looking for those who are after His heart, who will settle for nothing less than the joy of His presence!

When the battle lines were drawn, Saul had no strength. But David found the courage to run quickly toward the battle line because he knew his God! He knew what it meant to feel God's presence and listen to His voice.

Friend, I am telling you right now, all real courage comes from spending time with the Holy Spirit. If you want to walk in boldness and power to fulfill the assignment that God has placed in your life, you must get to know the precious person of the Holy Spirit. The secret place of prayer has always been where the power comes from, and there are no shortcuts.

You may not like this, but the truth is that David did not happen upon some kind of special giant-slaying anointing of courage. His confidence toward God was something that he had cultivated in those hours he spent with God in the pastures. He learned what it was to be with God, to sense God's approval, to receive His strength.

If you wait until the battle lines are drawn, you will have waited too late. Courage is something that is decided before there is ever a whisper of a fight. Courage is a posture that is learned from having total confidence in Jesus Christ, and you only learn it from spending time in prayer and in His Word.

So many people chicken out on God because they have not spent time getting to know Him. Confidence toward God is not something that you can get from standing in a prayer line to receive from a preacher. This isn't something you can get by sowing into someone else's ministry. You just have to show up and be with the Lord. You don't have to have all the right words. You have to have the right heart attitude that says, "Lord, I am here for You. I have come to minister to Your heart."

When I try to do something for God in my own strength, I have a 100 percent fail rate. When I wait on the Lord and stand by the power of His Spirit, I have a 100 percent success rate.

If you were to be honest, friend, I am certain you could say the same thing. We rise when we trust in God and we fall when we count on ourselves. We must learn to lean into God's presence and let Him infuse our life with courage.

Real courage always goes straight past your comfort zone and heads straight for the danger zone. Oh, I know you may not like that. No one really does. But if you wanted a safe, cozy, comfortable religion, Christianity was not the best choice you could have made. We are not called to live anything like what this world calls a normal life. We have been called out!

It takes extraordinary bravery to face the world we are living in. These times are so outrageous! The battle lines have never been more clearly defined than they are right now. Standing and speaking the truth of the Word of God has always meant that the speakers of truth would be ostracized and, in some cases, persecuted. But now, taking a stand for Christ and agreeing with His Word is more costly than it has ever been.

Paul told Timothy: *For the time will come when they will not endure sound doctrine; but wanting to have their ears tickled, they will accumulate for themselves teachers in accordance to their own desires, and will turn away their ears from the truth and will turn aside to myths. But you, be sober in all things, endure hardship, do the work of an evangelist, fulfill your ministry* (2 Timothy 4:3-5).

Does that sound like a cushy lifestyle to you? Paul was not telling Timothy how to be a great influencer. He was not telling him how to be relevant to the culture. He was telling him that living out the call of God on his life was going to be costly.

In the Western world, there is so much teaching that God is going to bless us, increase us, and promote us. I absolutely believe that God blesses His children, but I often wonder whether some of this teaching is really representative of the Jesus we claim to follow. If we are really called to follow Jesus, that cannot mean that we are going to fulfill the American Dream. We claim to believe that there is more to this life than having material possessions, but is that how we live? Can we really say that we are living in the light of eternity?

It's a disturbing thought, but really, our personal comfort in this life is not on God's priority list. "But Lydia, the Holy Spirit is the Comforter." Yes, He is, and I thank God that He is. The Holy Spirit can comfort like no one else can, and I have lived in that reality many times in my life. But the Holy Spirit will only comfort your spirit; He will never do anything to comfort your flesh. Do you know how I know that? Jesus Himself said that the only destiny of your flesh is the Cross! It's as though He was saying, "If you want to really be My disciple, you've got to deny yourself (your comfort), pick up your cross, and follow Me to the execution!"

There is nothing comfortable about facing a conflict, but friend, this is the conflict of the ages. The fight is not coming; we are in the middle of it right now! If you are a child of God, surely you must sense the urgency of living in the last days. There is no time for you to run from your God-given assignment. We need every believer living out their calling. We need all hands on deck!

Someone once said, "Everything you have ever wanted is on the other side of fear." Isn't that always the way it works out? Think of the account of David facing Goliath. David was just as anointed to be the king as he ever would be, but his actual kingship was on the other side of this fight and many others. He could not reign until he survived the battlefield. He could not take his seat of authority until he took a stand with courage.

God is looking for some battle-tested people who are not willing to back down under pressure. Where are the warriors who are willing to take a stand in this hour? Where are those who will sing the words of that old song, "The Cross before me, the world behind me. No turning back!"

We live in Florida, which means that sometimes we have to run away from hurricanes. I have lived in hurricane country for most of my adult life, and I don't get nervous about the smaller ones. But let me tell you, when meteorologists said that Hurricane Dorian was going to plow through the peninsula of Florida at a very strong category four in 2019, we packed up to visit my parents in Georgia. Of course, Dorian ended up hitting the Bahamas and missing our home, but Nathan and the boys and I ended up spending some time with my mom and dad.

Dad has been a pastor for such a long time. We were talking about the level of compromise in the Church at large, and Dad said something I will never forget. "Lydia, we have lived to see the days when the Church takes its cue from the world, and not the other way around." How have we allowed this to happen, when God has commanded us to "come out from among them (the world) and be separate"? I believe that the compromise of the Church has led to its cowardice. We have no spiritual backbone because we have given in to the culture around us more than we have surrendered to God. Like Saul, we have lived in disobedience, so we are powerless before Goliath. What can be done to return the strength, the courage of the Church?

God's people must return to holiness. We must repent. There is simply no shortcut around living clean before the Lord through the power of the Holy Spirit. We have to stop seeking our own comfort and start seeking our own crucifixion. We have to stop excusing ourselves for our spiritual laziness and cowardice. We have to allow the Holy Spirit to both convict and empower us to stand against the spirit of the age. Keith Green said, "This generation of Christians is responsible for this generation of souls on earth." Surely, we can all agree that we must stop pursuing selfish interests and start doing all we can to aggressively reach the lost.

I'm going to get into something right here for a moment that may bother you a bit, but I trust you picked up this book out of hunger for the Lord. If you will hear me out, I would love to help you.

Many times, I have heard preachers in our time say, "Our church is working hard to be relevant to this generation." Track with me right here. I understand that when a preacher says that, it is usually with good intentions. I am not mad at anyone, and I am not aiming at anyone. But could it be that in our efforts to be relevant, we have been trying to make people feel comfortable? Is that really a good objective? Does that goal reflect Christ's intentions for us?

When I am around backslidden people, they usually feel uncomfortable despite my efforts to be kind. You can see them squirming. Lost people are drawn to talk to saved people, but there is a difference in feeling welcome and feeling comfortable.

As a worship leader, I have had people tell me so many times that they didn't like a song that we chose. I don't mean any disrespect, but that never changes the way I choose songs. Why? It is because I do not choose songs to make church people feel comfortable. Worship time is God's time. My objective is for Him to be magnified, not for the congregation to feel comfortable. You may not agree with me, but let me remind you, the rest of the service is directed to people. I want people to be ministered to, but I am going to make sure that the songs I choose minister to the Lord. He must have the first priority.

I think that the saints of God ought to be a walking disturbance to the kingdom of darkness. When I read the book of Acts, I don't see the Church trying to be appealing to the world; I see separated ones living in extreme commitment to Jesus, willing to pay the ultimate sacrifice. Let's remember, that's the kind of church that God added to on a daily basis (see Acts 2:47). These people lived with such courage that in a time when there was no television or social media, they swept the known world with the message of Jesus Christ, even though most of them had to give their lives for that message. They reached beyond their comfort and grabbed on to commitment.

I love the story of Esther, the young Jewish lady who concealed her ethnicity and faith and became the queen of the Persian Empire. She rose to become the wife of the most powerful king of her time. Esther won the ultimate beauty contest. Her life is like the script of a princess movie, except this really happened. But she did not just become the queen; God expected her to do something where He placed her. She had not received a powerful position for her own sake. There was a purpose in her position.

Esther found herself right in the middle of a fight she had never asked for. Suddenly, she was being asked by her uncle Mordecai to speak to King Xerxes to try and stop the genocide against the Jews. It was an unthinkable predicament.

Protocol in the court of King Xerxes dictated that you simply did not come into his presence unless he sent for you. To approach him without being sent for meant that he would have to extend his scepter to you, which was a sign of his favor. If that did not happen, you would be executed. There would be no appeal.

At first, Esther felt that approaching the king was out of the question. Who could blame her? Everyone knew what an insane risk this was. Everyone knew that when the first queen went against protocol, the king had banished her. Esther had no reason to expect mercy, let alone favor. Mordecai was asking her to do something impossible.

The Bible records their conversation:

> *Then Mordecai told them to reply to Esther, "Do not imagine that you in the king's palace can escape any more than all the Jews. For if you remain silent at this time, relief and deliverance will arise for the Jews from another place and you and your father's house will perish. And who knows whether you have not attained royalty for such a time as this?" Then Esther told them to reply to Mordecai, "Go, assemble all the Jews who are found in Susa, and fast for me; do not eat or drink for three days, night or day. I and my maidens also will fast in the same way. And thus, I will go in to the king, which is not according to the law; and if I perish, I perish"* (Esther 4:13-16).

Would you imagine with me what it must have been like to have been the messenger who heard Esther speak those courageous words? The young queen, new to the job, knowing that she is likely going to die for who she is, speaks with an audacity that defies the protocol everyone else fears.

If maintaining the status quo of comfort is more important to you than speaking with the voice of courage, God will use someone else to do what you are supposed to do. Yes, there are specific assignments that God has for your life, but He can cause deliverance to come from any other source He chooses. But He wants to use you! He wants to hear courage coming up out of your spirit. He wants you to fulfill the good destiny that He has for you. Stop worrying about the risks and start stepping out in faith! You are not living the Christian life if you are still living for your comfort.

You see, real courage will fly in the face of the status quo that everyone has always accepted. Real courage will stand for what is right, even when it has to speak truth to power. There is something priceless about taking a stand when it could cost you everything.

Do you really want to have courage?

Oh, I pray that God will raise up men and women around the world who will stand with the boldness that Esther demonstrated in her generation! She saved the lives of God's chosen people by risking her own life and comfort. May the same be said of us today.

That kind of courage has only one source: the Holy Spirit. Only He can empower a life to speak with the voice of courage.

Sometimes, when I want to encourage myself, I look to the Word of God and to church history to see if I can find those who spoke with the voice of courage. These men and women of God moved past the comfort zone and boldly spoke for God and against the enemy. I want to briefly introduce you to a few of my favorites.

Joshua and Caleb stood together against ten other spies to say that Israel could take the land that God had promised them. In Numbers 13:25–14:9, the Bible indicates that the ten spies who did not agree with God brought back an evil report. They said that Israel could not take possession of what God had promised. I would love to have seen the moment when Caleb quieted the people and said, "*We should by all means go up and take possession of it, for we will surely overcome it*" (Numbers 13:30). He quieted the entire nation by agreeing with God and having the courage to speak out, even when the other ten spies were saying the opposite.

What if we came to a point in our faith where we have more confidence in God than we have in the culture around us? What would happen if we had the audacity to believe God and speak out with boldness? What if we took a stand to see a move of God in our lifetime?

Joshua and Caleb received an inheritance in the Promised Land, while no one else of their generation did. Could it be that courage is the ingredient that we need to inherit what God has destined for our lives?

You can only enter the fullness of the promises of God for your life when you respond to adversity with the voice of courage. Any other type of response will cause you to stop on the border of your destiny and die in the wilderness. Joshua and Caleb were not in denial about the presence of the enemy. They just had courage that came from confidence and trust in God. That's why they spoke with the voice of courage!

Hebrews 10:35-36 says, "*Therefore, do not throw away your confidence, which has a great reward. For you have need of endurance, so that when you have done the will of God, you may receive what was promised.*"

I want to be someone who receives what God has promised. I am so aware that one of the reasons I get to serve the Lord in full-time ministry is because of the way my parents and grandparents walked with God. I don't want to let them down for a moment. I want to stand with courage as they have done, because I want to walk in the fullness of the promise of God for my family.

I also hear the voice of courage when I look at church history and read the accounts of the martyrs. Their stories stir up my faith and make me want to take a stand.

One of my favorites is Polycarp, who was the bishop of Smyrna. He had been mentored by John the Beloved, and he himself had ministered faithfully for many years. When the Romans finally arrested him, John Foxe reports, "He prayed with such fervency, that his guards repented that they had been instrumental in taking him." But he was brought to the proconsul for his fate to be decided.

They gave the elderly Polycarp a chance to renounce Jesus Christ and have his life spared. He did not hesitate. He said to the Roman authorities, "Eighty and six years have I served him, and He never did me any injury: how then can I blaspheme my King and my Saviour?"[1]

What kind of courage do you think it would take to stand tied to the stake they intend to burn you on, while still proclaiming love for the Jesus they hate so much? They did try to burn Polycarp at the stake, but they found that the fire could not touch him. They had to kill him with the sword, and the blood that flowed from his body put out the flames. His voice never wavered. This man was filled with such boldness that he stayed true to Christ, even while paying for it with his life.

There was another leader in the early Church called Ignatius. He was also facing a martyr's death. This is what he had to say: "Now I begin to be a disciple. Not shall any thing move me whether visible or invisible, that I may attain to Jesus Christ. Let fire and the cross; let the companies of wild beasts; let breaking of bones, and tearing of members; let the shattering in pieces of the whole body, and all the wicked torments of the devil come upon me; only let me enjoy Jesus Christ!"[2]

Oh, Father, give us a fearless heart!

I have only mentioned two men who stood fast to the end of their earthly lives, but every day in nations around the world, people are standing true to Christ even though they know they will die for it. When I think of that, it makes my heart burn. I cannot fail to preach the unadulterated Gospel of Jesus Christ when I know that so many have poured out their very life's blood to preach it.

Throughout this book, I have reminded you that revival is not about us having more extended meetings; rather, it's about God pouring His Spirit out on all flesh, giving us the courage to speak the truth no matter what it costs us.

Have you yet experienced something in God that you would be willing to lay your life down for? We need a real revival remnant, a company of fearless people who reach beyond comfort and grab ahold of commitment to Jesus Christ and His Kingdom!

> *For the weapons of our warfare are not carnal, but mighty through God to the pulling down of strong holds* (2 Corinthians 10:4 KJV).

When we look at the way David fought Goliath, much of that story does not make sense in the natural. How is an untrained teenage shepherd boy supposed to fight a skilled warrior, especially when that warrior was somewhere between nine and thirteen feet tall? The boy throws a rock, fells Goliath, and then uses Goliath's own sword to end him. I believe this story exactly the way it is written, but, friend, this is not logical!

Many times, we want things to make sense in the natural before we step out in faith. We want to have all our ducks in a row. Everything just needs to be logical so that we aren't doing something risky. The problem with that way of thinking is that it removes the need for faith! We want things to be logical, but that is simply not the way God works.

I once posted something on Facebook that made some people mad. I'm going to include it now, so brace yourself.

> God is not logical; He is supernatural. God Himself is above our way of thinking, of processing, and He is not going to conform to our natural logic. If you'd like some Bible for that, check out Isaiah 55:8-9:
>
> > *For My thoughts are not your thoughts, nor are your ways My ways," declares the Lord. "For as the heavens are higher than the earth, so are My ways higher than your ways, and My thoughts than your thoughts.*

First Corinthians 2:14 says, "*But a natural man does not accept the things of the Spirit of God, for they are foolishness to him; and he cannot understand them, because they are spiritually appraised.*"

He is not logical, but He is supernatural! His way of doing things can even look ridiculous to the natural mind, but when we trust Him and follow His ways, amazing things begin to happen.

Just for a moment, I want us to take a look at some of the battle plans God gave in His Word. The way God fights His battles shows us what Heaven calls "logic." And it never makes sense from an earthly perspective.

I love to think about what it must have been like for Joshua to come to his generals and tell them the plan God had given him. Can you imagine it with me?

Joshua says, "Okay, guys, good news! God has given me a plan."

They say, "Let's hear it."

Joshua says, "Well, we're gonna walk around the wall once a day for seven days in total silence. No one is allowed to even say a word."

"Right...then what are we gonna do?"

"On the seventh day, we're gonna walk around the wall seven times. Then, the priests will blow the trumpets, and when I say 'Go!' we're all gonna yell at the top of our lungs."

Imagine the awkward pause in the room as those generals try to process the information. And Joshua says, "That's the plan; that is the whole plan. There is no backup plan. This is it."

To the natural mind, this plan was utterly ridiculous. You cannot walk around a wall to knock it down. Blowing a trumpet should not knock a wall down. Shouting should not conquer a fortified city. This battle plan makes no logical sense at all, but our God does not move according to our logic.

Let's take a look at one more battle plan. David had been fighting against the Philistines. David was accustomed to fighting them directly, but this time, God said to him:

> *You shall not go directly up; circle around behind them and come at them in front of the balsam trees. It shall be, when you hear the sound of marching in the tops of the balsam trees, then you shall act promptly, for then the Lord will have gone out before you to strike the army of the Philistines* (2 Samuel 5:23-24).

This may be the most bizarre battle plan of them all! What must it have been like for David and his army to hide out and listen for the sound of marching in the bushes? I'm sure they felt ridiculous.

I wonder how many times we have let fear tell us that everything has to be perfect before we do something great for God. How often have we held back, simply because what was going on in front of us just didn't seem logical to us?

You see, if you want to accomplish a natural goal, you should apply natural logic. But if you would like to do something supernatural, you are going to have to step over into the realm of hearing God's voice. You cannot fight a supernatural battle in a natural way.

If you are going to be a part of the last-days remnant who contends for revival, you had better get ready for people to think you are ridiculous. Even among other believers, your "radical faith" will be looked at as strange and excessive. But I would rather be a woman of faith pressing in for a move of God than to be a normal, lazy Christian. I don't want to just wait for something to happen; I want to pray it down right now!

The call to be a holy provocation is no easy call. When God placed this assignment on our lives, it changed everything in a moment. It clarified us. It refined us. Our circle of friends grew smaller, but we felt Heaven's approval.

I am inviting you to allow God to make you a holy provocation—to let Him use your life to provoke the Church toward revival and the lost toward repentance. I know that it won't be logical to people around you. This is a call that requires courage that comes from the Holy Spirit. I know that it will cost you. But I also know that if you will allow Him to, God will take your life and use it as a conduit of His Spirit to bring revival and awakening.

I want God to overtake your personal life. I want Him to arrest your family with His wonderful presence. I'm asking Him to set your church or ministry on fire with the flames of His Spirit. I'm praying for God to raise up a generation who will seek His face, who will cry out for awakening that brings transformation. Only then will we see the glorious Church without spot or wrinkle or any such thing, the Bride of Christ who has made herself ready for His return.

For the last time in this book, I want to invite you to pray with me.

> *God, in the name of Jesus, I ask You to make me a burning firebrand of revival. Give me the courage that can only come from Your Spirit. Make my life a holy provocation! Let every person I come into contact with be provoked to love Jesus. Make me like David, running quickly to impossible battle*

lines so that Your glory can be revealed in my life. I ask it in Jesus' precious name, amen.

ENDNOTES

1. *The Martyrdom of Polycarp,* Chapter ix, "Polycarp refuses to revile Christ."
2. *The Epistle of Ignatius to the Romans,* Chapter II verses 12-13.

ABOUT LYDIA S. MARROW

When Lydia Marrow was nearly twelve years old, she had a life-changing encounter with the Holy Spirit in the altars of the Brownsville Revival. After attending Bible school there, she went on to be the worship leader of Church of His Presence and the Bay Revival. After being so mightily touched in those two moves of God, Lydia lives with a passion to see the Church walk in the fullness of Pentecost and to see the lost encounter Jesus Christ. Whether Lydia ministers through preaching the Word or through leading worship, her goal is always to see the power and demonstration of the Holy Spirit. Lydia and Nathan Marrow currently lead Vanguard Ministries, ministering throughout the USA and the nations of the world. They reside in Florida with their two little boys, Malachi and Jeremiah.

For more information about Vanguard Ministries, please visit: www.vanguardministries.tv

Follow Lydia on social media @lydiasmarrow.

Made in the USA
Coppell, TX
09 February 2024

28808052R00125